Anne Scott-James

The Cottage Garden

ALLEN LANE

ALLEN LANE
Penguin Books Ltd
536 King's Road
London SW10 0UH

First published 1981
Copyright © Anne Scott-James, 1981

The List of Illustrations and Acknowledgements on pages 152–5
constitutes an extension of this copyright page

ISBN 0 7139 1243 4

Printed and bound in Great Britain by
William Clowes (Beccles) Limited,
Beccles and London

Colour separations by
Culvergraphics, Lane End,
Bucks.

For Osbert

Contents

ACKNOWLEDGEMENTS

I would like to thank Peter Stageman, Librarian of the Royal Horticultural Society Lindley Library, for kind and constant help with this book, and for giving permission to reproduce many plates from the Library. I must also thank his assistant, Brent Elliott, who became as involved in cottage-garden history as I am myself. I am also grateful to: Susan Rose-Smith of Penguin Books for indefatigable picture research; Elizabeth David, for allowing me to use her cookery library and herself selecting relevant books; Sandra Raphael for interpreting some of the old plant names; and Susan Allison for research, typing and moral support.

1

In Search of
the Cottage Garden

Hollyhocks, mignonette and roses round the door – the English cottage garden has achieved the status of a legend. For more than a century, English novelists have idealized the cottage garden as a paradise of scented flowers and honest husbandry going back to the garden of Eden. Foreign observers go further and allege that all English gardening, even that on the grandest level, is based on the cottage garden, with its exuberant planting of a catholic mixture of flowers. French geometry, Italian classicism, Japanese symbolism are all, they feel, uneasy aliens in Britain, the English genius deriving from our ancient tradition of country life.

None of this is quite true. The history of the English cottage garden is not nearly as old as we like to think, and it is difficult to find even the flimsiest record of a good cottage garden before the second half of the eighteenth century. Evidence before this is thin, and although one is entitled to guess what older cottage gardens looked like, it is important not to be over-romantic, and to distinguish guesses from facts.

What does one mean by a cottage garden? Certainly not just the garden of the farm labourer, who was for many centuries too poor, too ignorant and too badly housed to set a standard of cultivation. Cottage gardening is not a style of peasant origin. I think the term 'cottager' must be taken to embrace, from medieval times until the late eighteenth century, the small farmer or husbandman, the country craftsman, especially the blacksmith, who was the aristocrat of village artisans, and any servants of the gentry who 'lived out', perhaps gardeners or dairymen for whom there was no room in the manor house. These were all country cottagers, but there were also cottagers in towns, and one must include the town artisan, if he had his own small plot. Though all these gardeners were likely to be better off than the farm labourer, yet their gardens were for centuries planned for use rather than beauty. At best, the cottage garden would have livestock, vegetables and herbs and perhaps a few flowers for ornament and scent, and at worst it was a slum. Certainly it had to be managed as cheaply as possible, with minimal expenditure on tools and seeds.

It was not until the latter half of the eighteenth century that the poor man's garden had any status at all, and then landowners began to look at their cottages with new eyes. Some, drunk on the fashion for the picturesque, built *cottages ornés* to be pretty toys in the landscape, and others with more sense developed a social conscience about their tenants and taught them how to improve their garden plots. At the same period, many gentry of small means began to live in cottages themselves – in larger, better-built cottages than had been known before – and the cottage garden became increasingly a skilfully cultivated and much-loved home for both ornamental and edible plants. Pushed on by intellectuals and philanthropists, the cottage-garden movement gathered momentum all through the nineteenth century, and the cottage garden of our dreams, with its mixture of flowers and neat rows of nourishing vegetables, is largely a Regency and Victorian conception.

The Early Days

Not much is known about the medieval cottage garden, and one can only speculate on its size and shape, but there are occasional clues. My own guess is that it was more of a yard than a garden, and that animals were more important than crops. The poorest cottager might grow corn, beans and peas in an open strip or graze a few sheep on the common and have no garden at all attached to his wretched home-made hovel of timber, wattle and daub roofed with thatch. If he kept

An early cottage garden was just a yard.

chickens or a pig, they lived *en famille* inside the cottage. But the small farmer had a more substantial home – perhaps a cottage for the family and a separate barn at right angles to the cottage, forming the basis of a yard, so that it was a simple matter to complete the enclosure with a wattle fence or perhaps a thorny hedge.*

It is unlikely that the poor eked out their sparse diet, as we do today in hard times or in wartime, by growing many vegetables; at best the cottager might have a patch of leeks, onions, beans or cabbage. The English are a nation of carnivores, and have never eaten vegetables if they could get meat. In the Middle Ages, vegetables appeared but rarely on the rich man's table, were food for fast days in the monasteries, and were boiled down by the peasants into pottage. What the Englishman of every class liked best was animal food, and in prosperous times the cottager kept pigs and poultry and possibly a few sheep. Even if he had to sell the best part of his produce, he would still have a diet of coarse bread, milk, bacon, cheese, eggs and occasionally fowls or other white meat. He might have had a plum, apple, pear or cherry-tree in the yard, for fruit was widely grown in the Middle Ages, and he probably had beehives. But even if the cottager managed to preserve some fruit, his winter diet must have been seriously deficient in vitamin C.†

Though kitchen vegetables were monotonous and not popular, there was a wide range of herbs, used by rich and poor alike for physic, for flavouring and for scent. In the Middle Ages, and indeed for centuries afterwards, there was much home doctoring; remedies for illness were herbal and every housewife had a smattering of medicinal lore. If her husband cut himself with an iron tool she dressed the wound with yarrow pounded with grease, and if the children got whooping-cough she gave them juice of pennyroyal. She used herbs, too, to flavour her cooking, especially if the meat was going off or the pottage was a thin one made with a scanty handful of vegetables and water. The poor cottager's wife would not have much use for herbs for scent, but the farmer's wife might hang up bunches of sweet woodruff or strew the floor with meadowsweet to keep away fleas and lice. Most of the herbs

* Maurice Beresford and John G. Hurst (eds.), *Deserted Mediaeval Villages*, 1971.
† J. C. Drummond and Anne Wilbraham, *The Englishman's Food*, 1939.

were picked wild, but thrifty cottagers dug them up and brought them home to plant near the house, and they sometimes dug up and transplanted wild strawberries too.

So the medieval cottage garden was probably a fenced-in yard with a shed or two, and with subdivisions inside the yard so that the cow did not eat the herbs or the pig grub up the cabbages. There is a garden of this sort charmingly described in the Nun's Priest's Tale in *The Canterbury Tales*. Chaucer tells of a poor widow who supported herself and two daughters by husbandry. She had a fenced yard and kept three large sows, three cows, a sheep called Molly, a cock and seven hens, and the family lived tolerably well on brown bread, milk, roast bacon and eggs.

In addition to the animals, the widow had a 'bed of wortes', presumably coleworts or cabbages, in the yard, and a prolific herb patch. When Chanticleer, the splendid cock, went sick, his favourite wife, Partlet, diagnosed constipation, and prescribed a diet of two days on worms followed by a purge of herbs from the farmyard: spurge laurel, centaury, fumitory, elderberries, caper spurge, blackthorn berries and ground-ivy. I am afraid that all Chanticleer replied was 'Madame, gramercy for your lore,' and ignored her advice, but at least we know that the herbs were there, growing inside the cottage yard.

Probably the partitions inside the yard were easily movable wattles, so that patches of crops, like cabbages or beans, could be rotated with enclosures for the animals, and the ground could be regularly manured. Another important source of manure would be the mobile privy, which worked its way round the garden enriching the soil, so that even today we find the soil of very old gardens rich and black.

Queen Elizabeth and Merry England

In Tudor and Elizabethan times, the pattern of the humbler cottager's prosperity was highly erratic, and one cannot pretend that there was a steady improvement in his standard of living. He was at the mercy of politics, economics and the luck of the harvest, and in one decade he might have mutton and goose in his diet and in another be reduced to near starvation level, with bread made of flour adulterated with acorns.

(This fluctuation is true throughout our agricultural history, and in the farming depression of the 1880s the condition of many villagers was worse than in Chaucer's time.)

However, under Queen Elizabeth, the way of life of the upper and middle classes became more civilized than it had been since the Roman occupation and the prosperity trickled downward. In the cities, noblemen, gentlemen and merchants lived in luxury and kept the best table in the world, though their cooks were often foreigners who were artists at their trade – 'musical-headed Frenchmen', as one contemporary wittily expressed it. In the country, the big farmers were as rich as the gentry and built themselves comfortable mansions with lavish furnishings. Their dinner tables groaned with food, including Continental dishes. From the middle of the sixteenth century, they employed skilled gardeners and began to lay out decorative gardens in the formal Flemish style; new and improved flowers were grown in them, and a gourmet's range of vegetables and fruit. At last vegetables were appreciated as delicacies, not scorned as fodder for the poor, and they were grown in considerable variety.

Some of this rubbed off on the cottager, and out of the mists of the Middle Ages, a picture of the Elizabethan cottage garden comes into focus. Our best guide is a homely book of bad verse by a worthy gentleman called Thomas Tusser, who wrote *A Hundred Good Points of Husbandry* in 1557, a book of moral and practical precepts addressed to the tenant farmer and his wife. It was a best-seller and was later expanded to *Five Hundred Points* and ran into many editions, though how many farmers and their wives could read it remains a mystery.

Tusser tells us that the small farmer, or husbandman (and we are counting these as cottagers), had a garden distinct from his farm acreage, and that this was his wife's dominion, and that in it she grew many herbs and flowers. He also had an orchard.

The wife had a large range of plants to choose from when stocking her garden. Tusser recommended dozens of seeds and herbs for the kitchen, from parsley to primroses; more than twenty plants for salads and sauce, including artichoke, endive and violets; others to boil and to butter, including pompions (pumpkins), carrots and rounceval peas;

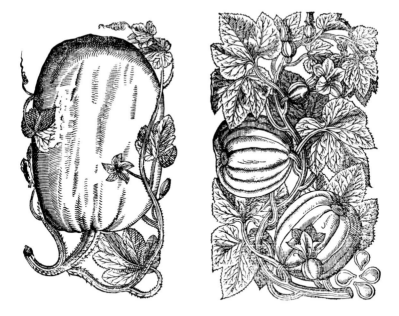

Pompions from Gerard's *Herball.*

twenty-one sorts of herbs for strewing on the floor to discourage lice and fleas, notably lavender and tansy; many herbs and fruits for stilling, including hops, roses, strawberries and sorrel, and for physic, including mandrake and rhubarb.

About forty flowers were suggested for windows and pots, that is, for purely decorative use, including columbines, carnations, roses, snapdragons, sweet williams, double marigolds, lilies, peonies, nigella and hollyhocks, many of which would be unimproved wild flowers of modest size and gentle colour. Tusser must have meant that some of these flowers could be grown in the flower garden and cut for vases in the house, for it is difficult to imagine a hollyhock grown as a pot plant. The range of fruit which the husbandman might cultivate now included peaches, strawberries, gooseberries and grapes.

This may sound more like a programme for the gentleman's rather than the cottager's garden, but Tusser makes it clear that the husbandman was a working farmer, and that both he and his wife had

15

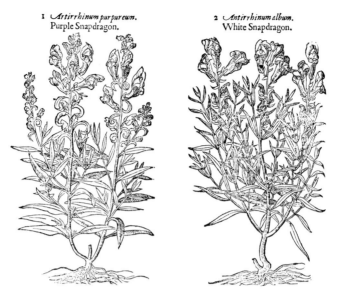

1 *Antirrhinum purpureum.*
Purple Snapdragon.

2 *Antirrhinum album.*
White Snapdragon.

Gerard's snapdragons.

to 'moile and toile'; so the Elizabethan farmer who worked hard could be a prosperous person and keep a good table. The housewife, though expected to remember God, make her husband happy, rise early, cook three meals a day, milk the cows, see to the dairy, bake, brew and still, and be a paragon of thrift, had pennies to spare for charity.

> Remember the children, whose parents are poore,
> which hunger, yet dare not crave at thy door.

Tusser does not tell us what the housewife's flower garden looked like, but any woman who cared enough about flowers to cut them for the house must have paid some attention to design. Almost certainly she would have grown her flowers in small formal beds in the Elizabethan manner, with the most useful kitchen herbs near the cottage door.

At this time, even the poor labourer enjoyed an expanded horizon. With the lord of the manor and the yeoman farmer creating ornamental and productive gardens, the more intelligent labourer must have picked up a few ambitions and tried to make his garden neater, to grow another crop or two, and perhaps to include some purely decorative flowers. We do not always make enough allowance for the powerful motive of imitation, and surely if Shakespeare's 'mechanicals' in *A Midsummer Night's Dream* could be stirred to produce a play they might also be inspired to erect an arbour covered with honeysuckle or to plant herbs in the pattern of a knot.

William Harrison, in his *Description of England*, written between 1577 and 1587, reported that both rich and poor grew many herbs, roots and fruits – pompions, gourds, cucumbers, radishes, parsnips, skirrets (perennial parsnips), carrots, cabbages, turnips, and all kinds of salads. Certainly, many villagers kept bees. Professor W. G. Hoskins, in *The Making of the English Landscape*, says that 1570 to 1640 was the great period when the modern village was made, when fine houses, better cottages and new schools and almshouses were built, and when rural England reached its finest flowering. His judgement is confirmed by Rowland Parker in *The Common Stream*; his minute researches, both in county records and in the field, prove that his village of Foxton in Cambridgeshire was completely rebuilt between 1550 and 1620.

New Crops, New Flowers

By the time of the publication of John Parkinson's *Paradisi in Sole, Paradisus Terrestris* in 1629, gardening had become a major recreation with the English upper classes, and men created gardens for pleasure and beauty. Though *Paradisi* is mostly about flowers, Parkinson also discusses fruit and vegetables, and the best ways of serving them. Some of his recipes are delicious, such as meat stuffed with onions and parsley, and globe artichokes boiled and dressed with oil and vinegar and a butter sauce. (Today we use one sauce or the other, but Parkinson liked both.) There is occasional mention of the poor man's garden, and Parkinson says that he 'grew all sorts of herbs, as roots and fruits, that are usually planted in gardens, to serve for the use of the table, whether of the poor or the rich', turnips, beans and the cheap, late varieties of peas for pottage being specialities of the poor – the poor seem to have been doomed for centuries to nourishing soups, but at least they flavoured them with thyme, mint, savory and other herbs. The poor also ate, and presumably therefore grew, radishes, which, according to Parkinson, 'do serve usually as a stimulum before meat; the poor eat them alone with bread and salt', in other words as a main meal, not an appetizer. Turnips were a speciality of 'poor men's feasts', being nourishing, though 'very windy'. Vegetable marrows were slit, de-seeded and baked by the poor in both city and country. One would like to think that the baked marrows were stuffed with mince or something meaty, but Parkinson does not say so.

This was a period when it was possible for country people to jump up a class. New men were making fortunes and investing money in land, so that rural England flourished, and better houses were built, farms were improved, and the poor had a little leisure. In many districts arable was replacing sheep farming, which meant more employment and better conditions for the villagers. Yeomen became gentlemen, small farmers became literate and tried to improve their properties, and the clever son of a craftsman could rise through education; the great botanist, John Ray, who went to a local Essex school and Cambridge, was the son of a village blacksmith. This was one of the happiest periods for the cottager.

Yet, of course, the prosperity was patchy. If in some districts villagers were dancing round the maypole, in others there was the same old poverty, and conditions so distressing as to stir, among intellectuals, a new spirit of philanthropy.

John Evelyn, founder of the Royal Society, was much concerned with the condition of the labourer and put forward the revolutionary proposal that the potato, with its high yield, might be a valuable garden crop for the poor and, in 1662, the Royal Society decided to investigate the possibilities, unfortunately with no immediate results. The reception of the potato in Britain was erratic. By Parkinson's time it was quite a delicacy on the rich man's table, and was sometimes cooked with spices, or even candied, but the conservatism of the labourer impelled him to refuse all offers of potatoes, even as a gift, and the potato did not become a common cottage crop until the end of the eighteenth century. The exception was in Ireland, where the starving,

The first potatoes.

war-weary poor seized on the potato as a staple food soon after its introduction at the end of the sixteenth century, but in their ignorance they grew it to the exclusion of almost all other crops, which was to bring tragedy later on. The potato was also adopted in Lancashire and other hungry northern English counties long before it reached the south.

The average English cottage garden remained a patch of old-fashioned vegetables, fruit and herbs, old-fashioned because the cottager could not afford the newest introductions, or did not like them. (Even today, few agricultural workers will look at a globe artichoke.) But certainly, the cultivation became increasingly skilful and the crops more plentiful, and most cottagers would grow a few flowers for pleasure as well as physic.

John Worlidge, in his *Systema Horticulturae*, of 1667, tells us that there was 'scarce a cottage in most of the southern parts of England, but hath its proportionate garden, so great a delight do most men take in it'. And he has a chapter on 'Vulgar Flowers', which are flowers grown 'for scent or shew' in ordinary country gardens and which 'every *colona* knoweth how to plant, sow or propagate'. It is clear that the *colona*, or farmer's wife, was in sole charge of the flower garden, as indeed she was in Thomas Tusser's day. Many of the flowers grown by the *colona* are wild-flowers, like crowfoot, marsh-marigold, toadflax, and foxgloves, but many double flowers are in his list (given in full in the Appendix on page 145), and were highly prized: pellitory, featherfew, chamomile, and so on. Worlidge also tells us that gardening was so popular that even a town shopkeeper, with no garden, grew flowers in boxes and pots.

The humbler cottager had many models to inspire him – the fine gardens of the gentry, the improved gardens of the yeoman farmers and, in certain parts of England, the well-run market gardens created by Flemish and French refugees, who traded in both vegetables and flowers. The French, the Flemings, and also the Italians, had always *liked* vegetables, and through the centuries when the well-to-do Englishman was gorging meat and game and the poor man was living on bread, cheese, eggs, pottage and as many scraps of meat as he could get, the foreigner had been growing improved vegetables and cooking them well.

The French and Flemish also brought with them their skill in growing 'florists' flowers'. A florist was a flower breeder who aimed at specimen blooms of great size and perfect shape. (The early meaning of the word has nothing to do with a flower-shop.) Such flowers need intensive cultivation but very little space, and selecting and improving them proved an infectious hobby for any cottager whose mind reached beyond the basic struggle to keep alive. Floristry became an important branch of cottage gardening, and will have a later chapter to itself.

It is safe to assume that by 1700 a good cottage garden would be skilfully cultivated, productive of well-grown vegetables and herbs, with several fruit-trees and a few flowers. These might be florists' auriculas or pinks, or native flowers like honeysuckle and primroses, and perhaps a showy clump or two of hollyhocks, crown imperials or lilies. And there would probably be bee plants, for though bees forage far afield and could get all their food from the plentiful wild-flowers in the open country, many beekeepers enjoy watching their bees at work near the hive and grow plants rich in nectar for the purpose.

But the hard evidence is scant. Gray's 'short and simple annals of the poor' is a wonderfully telling line. Travellers and historians simply took the rural poor for granted, and did not think their homes and gardens worthy of description.

2
The Eighteenth Century: Cottage Life Expands

Now at last the cottage garden enters more solid realms of history. In the eighteenth century, the rich and the gifted embarked on vast new rural projects which affected the cottager profoundly, sometimes for the better but often, tragically, for the worse. Landowners held their workers in such a stranglehold that the happiness or misery of the cottage family depended largely on the squire's character or whim.

The Enclosures

The first important change was the acceleration of the enclosure movement, which had been going on steadily for centuries, but was now officially sanctioned by private Acts of Parliament. Some landlords, as before, enclosed new land to increase their own agricultural wealth, but the birth of the landscape garden was a new stimulus to enclose. A fashion grew up for 'emparking', or the enclosure of a large estate in a decorative park, and often human interests were thrown to the winds. Looking at his estate as an exquisite piece of pastoral scenery, the landowner might say to himself 'those tumbledown cottages are an eyesore, I must pull them down'.

The results of this destruction were mixed. Sometimes the landowner felt that a model village might be a charming feature of his new arcadia, and from quite early in the eighteenth century model villages were built, usually outside the park gates, to be admired by the fashionable visitor on his way to the big house. Though the motive may have been selfish, the result was usually an improvement. The new cottages, though small, were at least new and not crumbling, and were built of better materials than the old wattle and daub, and some of them had generous gardens, large enough, if the cottager knew his business, to provide food all the year round. By as early a date as 1712 the Earl of Orford, First Lord of the Admiralty, had swallowed up a village in a new artificial lake in his park at Chippenham, Cambridgeshire, but he built a new village outside with pairs of brick-and-tile cottages with large outhouses and substantial gardens. He also gave the village a charity school.* Since the village would be quizzed by fashionable eyes, one can be sure that the gardens were well cultivated and of model neatness.

But not all the enclosures were so gracefully managed. Many landowners, greedy for land, would destroy a village and build nothing in its place. They either turned out the cottagers to become homeless paupers, or snatched their gardens and common rights, leaving them with no scrap of land for the fruit, vegetables and flowers to which they had become accustomed. In either case, it was a calamity for the cottager, for whom the palmy days of the seventeenth century were over.

Oliver Goldsmith, in an essay written in 1762 called *The Revolution in Low Life*, writes in heart-rending terms of a village of a hundred houses where the people were like one family, poor, but not desperately so, happy, with a thriving social life. They had 'neat gardens and well cultivated fields'. Then a *nouveau riche* from London bought the estate and planned to abolish the village, providing neither new homes nor compensation for the cottagers, who faced destitution. (It is frustrating that Goldsmith did not spare a few lines to describe the 'neat gardens' in detail – he could have filled a vast gap in our knowledge.) Eight years later he followed up this theme in *The Deserted Village*.

In searching for the cottage garden of the eighteenth century I am afraid one must be ruthless and forget the poverty and homelessness of many cottagers and think of the luckier ones. There were plenty of

* *Villages of Vision*, by Gillian Darley.

23

small farmers with productive gardens cared for traditionally with livestock, crops and flowers. There were artisans concentrating on florists' flowers for the show bench. There were cottagers who lived in the encouraging background of a model village, and others with humane landlords who preferred continuity to change. There were cottagers improving their gardens with the helping hand of the philanthropist. And there were gentry taking to cottage life for the first time.

Some of the evidence is no more substantial than memory, but so many writers of the early nineteenth century refer regretfully to the old-fashioned cottage garden as a vanishing delight that it must have existed – it must have been a happy and well-loved part of the scene in many parts of England. On the other hand, there is plenty of solid evidence about the florist's garden (see Chapter 6) and reliable contemporary writers have described the gardens of model villages towards the end of the century, the gardens of the minority of labourers blessed with good landlords, and the gardens of the gentry.

Model Villages

By the end of the eighteenth century there were model villages in various parts of Britain, and much aesthetic controversy as to how they should be designed. The earlier ones usually consisted of pairs of identical cottages lined either side of a village street, like Nuneham Courtenay, built in the 1760s. The gardens were rectangular and all the same. But a few decades later architects turned to more picturesque designs for villages, with quaint cottages and irregular gardens stuffed with plants – this ideal was expounded by Herefordshire squire, Sir Uvedale Price, in his book, *An Essay on the Picturesque* (1794), in which he discussed not only village design, but cottage gardens and their planting.

Price deplored the monotony of the Nuneham Courtenay linear type of village street. He suggested (and the more enlightened of today's planners would agree) that villages were prettier and more sociable built in the traditional way round a green, and that where possible an old village should be preserved as a nucleus, so that old fused with

1 (opposite). One of Gilbert White's favourite walks at Selborne took him past these neat cottages. S. H. Grimm painted them in 1776, as part of a series of Selborne water-colours commissioned by White himself.

2. Cottage life was not all tears and travail.
Thomas Rowlandson painted this robust rustic scene in the Isle of Wight.

3. Cottage crafts and cottage animals, notably pigs,
but no attempt at cultivation, in a painting by Francis Wheatley.

4. A more sophisticated cottage garden with pots of flowers. Paul Sandby painted his own studio and garden at Englefield Green, Surrey, in 1746.

5. A large cottage has a useful yard with well, sawing-horse and pigsty, and rudimentary planting on the house. Painted in 1806 by Cornelius Varley.

6 . By 1816 many painters and writers, including the Wordsworths,
were living in superior cottages. This was the view, before and after 'improvement',
from the Essex cottage of the famous landscape gardener, Humphry Repton.

new. He thought the cottages should be varied in style, but that all should have elaborate chimneys and porches and should be picturesque. Some built at this time were cloyingly pretty, though the heights of gingerbread taste were not reached until a little later; Blaize Hamlet, built by Nash and Repton in 1810 round a green near Bristol, is the ultimate fairy-tale village, and should house Snow White and the dwarfs.

Price gives a clear picture of the romantic cottage garden he favours, combining beauty with utility and allowing a certain wildness. He suggests, as a delightful frame for a cottage, a large tree 'embracing' it with its branches, perhaps an acacia, a pine or a cedar to shade part of the house. There are to be climbing plants up the trees, festooning them – a foretaste of William Robinson – and honeysuckle, vines or jasmine are to clamber over the porch. Fruit-trees may be trained against the house wall, providing both ornament and a crop. There are to be other fruit-trees in the garden, and all is to be enclosed by a neat hedge. Price says, shrewdly, that neatness and regularity are always pleasing on a small scale. I was formerly inclined to dismiss Sir Uvedale Price as an absurd dilettante, possibly because he is usually paired, like Tweedledum and Tweedledee, with another less gifted Herefordshire squire, his friend Richard Payne Knight, but on searching for the origins of the great cottage gardens of the nineteenth century, I have come to realize the influence and stature of this apostle of the Picturesque.

Philanthropy

Price was an aesthete and though he was not indifferent to 'the comforts and enjoyments' of the cottagers, his book lacks the glow of philanthropy. However, in other circles, social morality had arrived. It was not yet the sickly, selfish patronage of the Victorians, who used social benefits as a means of keeping the lower orders in their place. A sound, practical eighteenth-century movement had for some years been under way to better the lot of the rural poor, a foundation on which John Claudius Loudon was to build a great edifice thirty years later.

The authors of this movement believed that a responsible cottager should have a freehold house and garden which, properly managed, perhaps with a loan to start him off, could support his family in reasonable comfort. And they proved it could be done and *was* being done in exceptionally favourable circumstances. One of the most moving early descriptions of a cottage garden is found in a little pamphlet written in 1797 by a certain Thomas Bernard, called *Account of a Cottage and Garden near Tadcaster*. At a time when there was much misery in cottage life there was also, in patches, rare contentment. The pamphlet starts like the opening of a novel.

> Two miles from Tadcaster, on the left-hand side of the road to York, stands a beautiful little cottage, with a garden that has long attracted the eye of the traveller. The slip of land is exactly a rood, inclosed by a cut quick hedge; and containing the cottage, fifteen apple-trees, one green gage, and three wine-sour plum trees, two apricot-trees, several gooseberry and currant bushes, abundance of common vegetables, and three hives of bees; being all the apparent wealth of the possessor.

The whole garden was beautifully neat.

The owner, called Britton Abbot, had gone to work as a farm-lad at

Britton Abbot's cottage near Tadcaster.

the age of nine, and was now sixty-seven. When young, he saved money, married, rented a cottage with two acres and common rights, kept two cows, and had seven children. All went well for nine years, when the land was enclosed and all his property taken away, and he had to look for a new home. Abbot then applied to a Squire Fairfax for a bit of ground by the roadside, and promised, if the land was granted, that 'he would show him the *fashions* on it'. Mr Fairfax gave him his plot – a rood, or a quarter of an acre – and he built his cottage with the help of neighbours.

He was a born gardener. His first step in making the garden was to plant round the plot a single row of quickthorn which, with admirable patience, he cut down six times successively when it was young so that it grew into a thick, flawless hedge – a lesson to those of us who plant a hedge for swift results. Inside he planted fruit-trees and bush fruit, his crop later bringing in from £3 to £4 a year. His potato crop averaged forty bushels annually, and he grew many other vegetables in military rows. The squire was so pleased with it that he abolished the rent, and Abbot, when thanking him, said that if more squires would find land for their labourers there could be good cottage gardens everywhere and fewer farm workers enduring the squalor and misery of the workhouse. The author of the pamphlet concludes by proposing a national scheme for cottage plots of a rood apiece, with the possibility of loans, tax exemptions and the provision of extra land for keeping a cow.

It is clear from this pamphlet, and from other sources, that a good relationship between squire and labourer was rare enough to be a matter for surprise, and that the working-class cottager was usually faced with the gardener's worst enemy – insecurity of tenure. Who, if his land may be snatched away in a moment, is going to indulge in the long-term planting which makes a garden something richer and more satisfying than an allotment?

The Gentry Move In

I said earlier that I do not think of cottage gardening as a folk art. (Floristry is the one aspect of it which might be considered working-class, a speciality of the tradesman or artisan.) The idea of romantic simplicity, of usefulness wedded to charm, came from sophisticated people, and in the last quarter of the eighteenth century quite a few gentry, usually impoverished, either built themselves cottages or enlarged and improved old ones, and became enthusiastic gardeners.

Their efforts were often ludicrous, and they had no notion of economy, but yet it was they who made the cottage garden great.

One pathetically incompetent gentleman cottager was Fanny Burney's husband, the French aristocrat, M. d'Arblay, a refugee from the French Revolution. The d'Arblays had no money, and after their marriage in 1793 they took to cottage life. M. d'Arblay drew up a plan for their first garden and tried to work it himself. But, as Fanny wrote to her father:

> Seeds are sowing in some parts where plants ought to be reaping, and plants are running to seed while they are thought not yet at maturity. Our garden, therefore, is not yet quite the most profitable thing in the world; but Mr d'A. assures me it is to be the staff of our table and existence.
>
> A little, too, he has been unfortunate; for, after immense toil in planting and transplanting strawberries round our hedge, here at Bookham, he has just been informed they will bear no fruit the first year, and the second we may be 'over the hills and far away!'
>
> Another time, too, with great labour, he cleared a considerable compartment of weeds, and when it looked clean and well, and he showed his work to the gardener, the man said he had demolished an asparagus bed! M. d'A. protested, however, nothing could look more like *les mauvaises herbes*.
>
> His greatest passion is for transplanting. Everything we possess he moves from one end of the garden to another, to produce better effects. Roses take place of jessamines, jessamines of honeysuckles, and honeysuckles of lilacs, till they have all danced round as far as the space allows . . . .
>
> Such is our horticultural history. But I must not omit that we have had for one week cabbages from our own cultivation every day! Oh, you have no idea how sweet they tasted! We agreed they had a freshness and a *goût* we had never met before. We had them for too short a time to grow tired of them, because, as I have already hinted, they were beginning to run to seed before we knew they were eatable.

There is much of Mr Pooter here. This was the d'Arblays' first garden, but they had no better luck with their second. M. d'Arblay was in ecstasy at the prospect of 'cabbage walks, potato beds, bean perfumes, and peas blossoms', but the poor man was unfortunately prone to disaster.

> M. d'Arblay has worked most laboriously in his garden, but his misfortunes there, during our absence, might melt a heart of stone. The horses of our neighbouring farmer broke through our hedges, and have made a kind of bog of our meadow, by scampering in it during the wet; the sheep followed, who have eaten up all our greens, every sprout and cabbage and lettuce destined for the winter, while the horses dug up our turnips and carrots; and the swine, pursuing such examples, have trod down all the young plants, besides devouring whatever the others left of vegetables. Our potatoes, left, from our abrupt departure, in the ground, are all rotten or frost-bitten, and utterly spoilt; and not a single thing has our whole ground produced us since we came home. A few dried carrots, which remain from the indoor collection, are all we have to temper our viands.

The author of *Evelina* had not lost the comic power of her pen.

Much more successful with their cottage gardening were the two extraordinary Irish ladies who ran away together from their aristocratic homes in Kilkenny in 1778 and took a cottage in Wales where they spent the rest of their lives. They became known as the Ladies of Llangollen and their story is told in a brilliant biography by Elizabeth Mavor.

Eleanor Butler and Sarah Ponsonby settled in Plas Newydd, Llangollen, in 1780. It was a square stone cottage with five rooms in four acres of land, so that it was a small farmhouse rather than a labourer's cottage, in romantic hilly country with a mountain stream. Here the Ladies planned to live a life of retirement dedicated to friendship, study and the arts, and to the making of a perfect home and garden. Their little property was to be both useful and beautiful, with stable, dairy, poultry, vegetables, fruit and vines as well as the choicest shrubs and flowers of the day. Unfortunately, they were poor, a disadvantage with which they never came to terms, and they overspent from the very beginning to the end, which came fifty years later, and they were always in debt.

The cottage at Plas Newydd in 1810, with Gothic embellishments.

The Ladies were the apotheosis of eighteenth-century romantic thought. Everything in their lives was to be ideal, and much of the ideal was realized. They read prodigiously and learned languages, they walked among the hills and woods and studied nature, they sketched and embroidered, they remodelled their cottage, turning it into a *ferme ornée*, and they idolized their garden. (The first *ferme ornée* to be made in England is attributed to Philip Southcote, who designed a model farm at Chertsey in the Thames valley in 1735; the farm was a real one, but was surrounded by an ornamental walk with ruins, Gothic buildings, seats and bridges to delight the visitor.)

As the years went by, the Ladies' taste developed from the romantic to the extravagantly picturesque and I am afraid that by 1815 or thereabouts they had pretty well ruined the place with fantastical Gothic adornments. Nor was 'the simple life' achieved by the genuinely simple method of doing it yourself. A gardener, footman, maids and outside workmen were employed, or more truthfully sweated, as they often had to whistle for their wages. However that may be, the Ladies had within a few years of their arrival at Plas Newydd quite ceased to be secluded and had become famous throughout Europe, their home a point of pilgrimage to which cultivated travellers flocked, Mrs Piozzi, Wordsworth and Sir Walter Scott among them.

But in spite of the Ladies' celebrity their garden, though elaborately altered and frequently expanded, was always thought of by visitors as a cottage garden. Delightful as were the walks and shrubberies, vegetables and livestock always held an honoured place.

When the Ladies bought the cottage, there was a narrow belt of shrubs and a fence in front of it, and beyond the fence, a stretch of pasture for sheep. Within a few years, they had circled the whole garden with a wavy, shaded, gravel walk stopping at points of interest on the way, such as the model dairy, the poultry yard, and the various enclosures for flowers, vegetables and fruit. They had planted many trees and shrubs – limes near the cottage for sitting and dining under, thickets of flowering shrubs like lilac, syringa, laburnum, and broom. They were always planting new shrubberies, and they even altered the stream.

They made flower borders so richly planted that they included all the best flowers grown at the Kilkenny mansions in which they were born, including dahlias and geraniums in great variety, beds of carnations and luscious roses. But they also collected and brought home wild-flowers from the woods; there were wild gentians, primroses, strawberries, Snowdon pinks, huge white violets and drifts of snowdrops.

The vegetable garden, which was walled and had gravel paths and a rustic arch, included mushrooms and asparagus, melons and vines, strawberries and peas, all of the finest varieties, and visitors noted that there was not a weed to be seen. The Ladies made (or supervised) their own wine, preserves, dairy produce and bread.

As the years went by, they became increasingly interested in wild gardening, and this is the only point on which I would venture to question their biographer's conclusions. Elizabeth Mavor says that their wild garden was 'akin to the wild gardens of Francis Bacon, Batty Langley or Gertrude Jekyll. A purely English inspiration, it was a retreat from the excessive formality of the French gardens, and at its best it was a terrestrial Paradise, beautiful as it was romantic.'

But one of the Ladies' favourite books was Rousseau's high-flown novel, *Julie: ou La Nouvelle Helöise*, and Julie (a sickeningly sweet romantic heroine) had a wild garden more truly natural than anything envisaged by Bacon or Batty Langley. It was a hidden wood to which only four people had the key, and which the gardeners were allowed to enter on only a few days every year. There was no symmetry, no evidence of cultivation, no florists' flowers, just mossy glades of old apple-trees, hazels, flowering shrubs, wild-flowers and grass. The trees were unpruned and garlanded with wild hop and honeysuckle, and the stream and pond were overgrown with grasses, rushes and weeds. Still more remarkable was the fact that Julie's Elysium, as she named it, was treated as a wildlife preserve. Julie used to go every day to scatter grain for the innumerable birds who gathered there, and in spring she put down little heaps of hair, straw, wool and moss for their nests. The birds were guests, not prisoners as in an aviary; no bird's egg was touched nor nestling disturbed, and the children, allowed there as an occasional treat, were told to be quiet and gentle – this at a time when our own Gilbert White thought nothing of collecting rare species of birds for stuffing. Julie's Elysium must surely have inspired the Ladies when planning their thickets underplanted with wild flowers; they even chose some of Julie's shrubs, lilac, syringa and broom.

With Plas Newydd, we have strayed a long way from the simple cottage gardens of the husbandman, craftsman or labourer for which we have been searching. The Ladies' garden was in the most exquisite aristocratic taste. Yet, their friends always considered the Ladies as cottagers and their house as a cottage, and so must we. From the latter part of the eighteenth century on we must recognize two streams of cottage gardening. There is the cottage gardening of the gentry, who always employ a gardener, but have a certain simplicity in their ideals, enjoying the sight of homely things, like vegetables, beehives and butter-churns, growing many hardy flowers and loving wild-flowers inside the garden hedge. And there is the cottage gardening of the poor, who must grow to eat but who learn much, as time goes on, about the cultivation of flowers, and about decorative features in the garden.

Sometimes, in places where the social gap narrows, the two streams meet, and we find perfect cottage gardens, both charming and productive, neat where neatness looks best (trim hedges, symmetrical vegetables) but with wilder corners where old-fashioned hardy plants and simple annuals are allowed to mix and ramble in profusion.

3

The Two Streams Meet

The year 1800 always seems to me to be the beginning of modern times. The characters in Jane Austen's novels are people we know. Byron's witty iconoclasm is much to our taste. Cobbett's radical thinking is in tune with our social attitudes. Class barriers begin the long, slow process of breaking down. And in the first quarter of the nineteenth century our subject, the cottage garden, moved from its infant struggles to maturity – by 1825 the cottage garden of our dreams had arrived. In many villages, the two streams of cottage gardening, romantic gardening and subsistence gardening, had met, and both gentry and labourers were making glorious small gardens to delight the eye and fill the kitchen basket. Linked by their common interest, the two classes met on level terms to talk gardening, to exchange cuttings and seeds, and to adopt each other's methods and plant mixtures. (Of course, in backward districts, there was no such happy coalescence, but more of this later.) By this date we know clearly what the cottage garden looked like.

Garden Plans

There were two classic ground-plans; probably both went back a long way in history, and both survive all over England today.

The first typical plan was where a cottage was built close to the road or lane, when it had a narrow front garden bounded by a hedge or fence, devoted to flowers, and a larger back garden for vegetables, bush fruit, animals, muck-heap, water-butt and privy. The small front garden was sometimes called the forecourt. Since the cottage windows were within a few feet of the passers-by, there was likely to be a good show of pot plants on the sill.

The other typical plan was where a cottage was set further back from the road, and then there was a central path leading to the cottage door. The main garden was in front of the house, and the centre path was usually bordered with flowers, and vegetables were planted behind the flowers in rows. There were also flower-beds under the windows. Muck-heap, pigsty, privy and so on were if possible tucked behind the house.

With either plan, there would be fruit-trees in convenient sunny places, a mass of climbers on the house, and often a neat row of beehives. Many cottagers would have their own well or pond.

Though these are, as it were, the classic shapes, any number of variations would be found within a single village. At the picturesque village of Blaize Hamlet, near Bristol, designed by Repton and Nash, all nine cottages and their gardens were deliberately planned to be of different shapes and aspects, but an older village, where cottages had been run up higgledy-piggledy, with gardens of rectangular, tri-angular, or wholly random proportions, might see just as much variety. The size would vary, too. The experts of the early nineteenth century held that the optimum size was a rood, or a quarter of an acre, but many cottagers had much more, and could keep livestock on a generous scale.

Some of the best cottage gardens in England were in Hampshire, according to several impeccable witnesses. First, we have Miss Mitford of Three Mile Cross, author of *Our Village*, written between 1824 and 1832, her subject not one village but an amalgam of many of the Hampshire villages she knew well. She describes in detail the cottage gardens of the gentry, the farmers' wives, the village craftsmen and all the other country people. Her testimony is borne out a few years later (1838) by William Howitt, writing in *The Rural Life of England* of the idyllic cottages of the New Forest, 'almost buried in the midst of their orchard trees and thatched as Hampshire cottages only are ... little paradises of cultivated life'. Howitt, an admirer of Cobbett, had travelled all over England and Scotland observing country life with keen radical eyes, and thought Hampshire the happiest county.

Our Village

In *Our Village* there were cottage gardens of all shapes and sizes, some facing on the village street, others in small irregular clusters round the common. Most were beautifully kept, though a few black sheep let down the standard – the poacher's garden was a squalid slum.

A retired publican lived in a tidy, square red cottage with a long, well-stocked garden beside the road. The publican, greatly bored by retirement, destroyed wasps' nests for all the parish, and even helped his wife with the housework. Next door was a shoemaker, with another long garden ending in a yew arbour. The blacksmith, a pugnacious man given to the bottle, had a gloomy, sunless dwelling with no garden to speak of.

However, next door to him was 'a spruce brick tenement, red, high and narrow, boasting, one above another, three sash-windows, the only sash-windows in the village, with a clematis on one side and a rose on the other'. It was the home of a woman with several jolly children.

The mason lived on the other side of the lane in a pretty white cottage in a garden full of flowers. His wife, who came of a long line of gardeners, grew chrysanthemums and dahlias of prize quality. Then there was the cottage of an officer and his family, covered with vines. These were on the main village street, but there were plenty of cottages further out in the country, just as well-stocked and well-kept.

Hannah Bint's vine-covered home was something of a smallholding. There was a flower garden, but also an Alderney cow, ducks, chickens, geese, pigs and bees, on which Hannah, a young girl whose father was crippled and whose mother had died, contrived to keep the family.

The mole-catcher lived on the edge of a wood in 'a snug cottage of two rooms, of his own building, surrounded by a garden cribbed from the waste, well fenced with quickset, and well-stocked with fruit-trees, herbs and flowers'. The cottage was thatched and an apple-tree spread over the roof. A long row of beehives extended along the warmest side of the garden; a pig occupied a commodious sty at one corner; and large flocks of ducks and geese, when not feeding on the green, enjoyed a roomy shed in the back garden which was larger than the cottage itself. The mole-catcher's healthy geese and ducks were always attacking the sickly birds of a poor old crone who lived next door, an endless source of conflict.

One cottager was a florist, a farmer's wife who kept peacocks, turkeys, wild duck and guinea-fowl in addition to more humdrum poultry. Like all florists, she cultivated speciality flowers of the finest possible shape and rarest colour, and she grew unusual plants and knew their Latin names.

Just as pretty in a different way was the rat-catcher's cottage, originally built as a picturesque *point de vue* to be seen from the local great house, a cottage 'copied from some book of tasteful designs for lodges or ornamented cottages ... smacking of the pencil and the engraver', but now a village shop in which the rat-catcher was a lodger. It was a self-consciously rustic building, with a yew-tree to one side and walls covered with climbers.

Two more cottages in *Our Village* call for special attention. One was a Gothic *cottage orné* a few miles from the village for which Miss Mitford felt nothing but contempt – it is an error to think that she viewed all village life sentimentally, for she was often sharp. It was 'a cot of spruce gentility' with an absurdly grand garden, a 'unique bijou' according to the estate agents, but in fact jerry-built. It was sited on the foundations of a real labourer's cottage, so that the rooms were small and damp, and though the builders had devised all sorts of ornate details, they had forgotten to put in a staircase. The garden, though tricked out with conservatories, roseries, ponds, rustic seats, Gothic dairies and all the other fripperies of the Picturesque, had allowed no space for crops or livestock. Rosebank was one of those cottages where tenants come and swiftly go.

The other important cottage was Miss Mitford's own, a 'cottage – no – a miniature house, with many additions, little odds and ends of places, pantries, and what not; all angles, and of a charming in-and-outness; a little bricked court before one half, and a little flower-yard before the other; the walls, old and weather-stained, covered with hollyhocks, roses, honeysuckles, and a great apricot-tree'. Stocks, carnations and geraniums grew in the forecourt, and behind the house was a garden room with one side made entirely of glass which served both as a greenhouse and as a sunny place in which to take breakfast and look out at a garden stuffed with flowers, simple and exotic, orderly and rambling, brilliant and delicate-hued, all the flowers of the cottage garden of that time.

The Plants They Grew

Taking the writings of Miss Mitford and William Howitt together, one gets a good picture of the plants grown in the many neat, fertile Hampshire villages. The only lacuna is in the vegetable section, where one must assume that all the common vegetables were grown, for Miss Mitford refers to them only once, and then, not surprisingly, it is our old friend the onion, the staple vegetable for hundreds of years, which merits her notice.

Trees and Shrubs

Many cottagers planted, or inherited, one small tree to shade and shelter the house and garden. One farm had a belt of hollies round the property. Sometimes there was an old apple-tree or a yew by the house. Boundary hedges were most often of quickthorn. Many gardens had an arbour, arched or cut like a sentry-box, of yew or privet. One must assume some flowering shrubs, certainly lilac and myrtle, and in some sheltered corners there was a bay-tree.

Climbers

The planting of climbers on cottages is a custom with a very old history, and the Hampshire cottages were no exception. Vine and honeysuckle held pride of place, but there were also, in the village, climbing roses, trained fruit-trees, clematis, convolvulus, jasmine, passion-flower and ivy, often wreathing the porch and climbing to the chimneys. Everlasting pea is not mentioned by Miss Mitford, but it would certainly have been there. This habit of smothering a cottage with climbing flowers and fruit has never gone into abeyance. Climbers like honeysuckle were also allowed to climb up fruit-trees in the manner praised many years later by William Robinson, Miss Jekyll and V. Sackville-West.

The vines or wall-grapes which smothered so many cottages in the south of England at this time were beautiful and productive plants and it is extraordinary that they are so little grown today. There were at least two dozen named varieties, all completely hardy in the south, some suitable for the table, some best for wine, some useful for both purposes; some were black, others white, some fruited early and others in late October. The oldest and one of the best was a fine black grape called The Miller, and the most reliable white wall-grape was held to be White Muscadine. These vines require careful planting, patience for a few years, since you must cut them back annually until you have a strong stock, and thereafter a little regular attention in the way of training and snipping off the shoots above the clusters.

Hardy Plants

Ever since the days when peasants brought herbs into their gardens from the wild, hardy plants have been the staple of the cottage garden. In the early days they were all English natives, but many improved flowers and foreign flowers were common in cottage gardens long before Miss Mitford's time. Some, indeed, which had gone out of fashion in grand gardens with the landscape movement, were fortunately preserved in cottage gardens.

In Miss Mitford's garden, there was a fine show of hardy flowers, but as she was on intimate terms with many village friends, she certainly gave much away and received treasures in return, so that the richness was spread.

Hollyhocks were grown in nearly all the gardens, and so were roses; there were also campanulas, peonies, pinks, whole borders of lily of the valley, Michaelmas daisies and polyanthus. Of the many annuals grown, none is more frequently and lovingly mentioned in nineteenth-century literature than mignonette, closely rivalled by stocks, which were often planted under the windows to scent the rooms; there were also sweet peas and larkspurs. (The sweet peas, it must be remembered, were not the large-flowered, frilly sort grown today, which date back only to 1900, but were small-flowered, often bi-coloured, and richly scented.) Of bulbs, lilies of all sorts, including tiger-lilies, were most highly praised, but tulips, crocuses and snowdrops were plentiful.

Bedding Plants

The favourite bedding plant of *Our Village* was the geranium, grown both in pots in the house and out of doors, but there were also splendid dahlias, wallflowers, China asters and Brompton stocks. It is a sign of the assured taste of those cottage gardeners that they did not see hardy

Geranium, a favourite pot plant.

plants and bedding plants as waging perpetual war, but enjoyed both. In her own garden Miss Mitford had

> a splendid pyramid of geraniums. Such geraniums! It does not become us poor mortals to be vain – but, really, my geraniums! ... This pyramid is undoubtedly the great object from the greenhouse; but the common flower-beds which surround it, filled with roses of all sorts, and lilies of all colours, and pinks of all patterns, and campanulas of all shapes, to say nothing of the innumerable tribes of annuals, of all the outlandish names that were ever invented, are not to be despised even beside the gorgeous exotics which, arranged with the nicest attention to colour and form, so as to combine the mingled charms of harmony and contrast, seem to look down on their humble compeers.

The geranium 'pyramid' lived in the garden room in winter and was moved outside in summer, so it must have been some large kind of frame for holding pots.

Here was a garden planted with 'the cottage mixture' in all its glory.

Florists' Flowers

The country cottage garden is not usually associated with floristry. Many of the important florists' societies, though by no means all, were based in the north of England, near the manufacturing centres. Here, the weavers and other cottage operatives found the growing of flower specialities, often for the show-bench, a relaxation from their repetitive work.

However, even in rural villages there were enthusiasts who devoted themselves to this kind of gardening, and the farmer's wife in *Our Village* was

> a real, genuine florist: valued pinks, tulips and auriculas for certain qualities of shape and colour, with which beauty has nothing to do; preferred black ranunculuses, and gave in to all those obliquities of a triple-refined taste by which the professed florist contrives to keep pace with the vagaries of the bibliomaniac. Of all odd fashions, that of dark, gloomy, dingy flowers appears to me the oddest. Your true connoisseurs now shall prefer a deep puce hollyhock to the gay pink blossoms which cluster round that splendid plant like a pyramid of roses!

But the offending farmer's wife also had a patch of which Miss Mitford did approve, a bee garden near the hives filled with scented flowers for the bees' use.

Fruit and Vegetables

Apples, pears, cherries, plums, apricots, strawberries and gooseberries are all mentioned in *Our Village* as familiar things, but vegetables unfortunately are not deemed worthy of notice. But they were certainly grown in abundance, as we can tell from a passing reference to onions.

> Dame Simmons makes an original use of her pond. Most ingeniously watering her onion-bed with a new mop – now a dip, and now a twirl. . . . It

is as good an imitation of a shower as one should wish to see in a summer day. A squirt is nothing to it.

Other fruit and vegetables which would certainly have been grown are raspberries, currants, leeks, root crops, cabbages, beans, peas, potatoes, lettuces and other salads and useful herbs. And there were a few melons, grown even by the poor – a pathetic, handicapped pensioner had three miserable melon-plants under a hand-light. He must have seen melons growing in a frame in some prolific garden, and been moved to try himself.

The Livestock

The range of domestic animals kept depended, of course, on the size of the garden. In a small garden, there was always a pig, certainly some poultry, and often bees. Cottagers with more land could keep a cow and extra poultry. The pig was the staple of cottage economy all through the nineteenth century, just as it had been in the Middle Ages. The pig provided manure for the garden as well as food for the family, but it had to be fed, and enough vegetables or cereals had to be grown to fatten it up, while gleaning and the collection of scraps would eke out its diet, a never-ending job for the cottager's children. Fortunately, the parish described by Miss Mitford had escaped enclosure, so that there were still open commons where, with permission from the landlord, geese could feed, and on the ground under a great avenue of oaks the pigs could be led to snuffle up acorns.

Through the Eyes of John Clare

Miss Mitford has delayed us long in Hampshire, for few observers of wild flowers and country gardens were so sensitive and exact. But other writers of her period described cottages of equal charm in quite different parts of England.

John Clare, the labourer-poet, wrote of the lovely little gardens of Northamptonshire. Although poor Clare was a melancholic, and much of his verse is lamentation, he shows us as well the cheerful side of village life, and 'merry' is a word he often uses. There were fairs and fêtes in his village society, parties at Christmas, good food and drink,

Trained fruit-trees, beehives, a few flowers, in 1834.

wooing and marrying, and deep happiness in both natural beauty and the comforts of a simple home. In some of the labourers' cottages there were brass fire-irons and warming-pans, scrapwork screens, grandfather clocks, decorated picture-frames – and even a few books. Home-made wine was brewed, herbs were dried for medicine, pigs and poultry filled the yard, there were blazing log fires in winter and evergreens were cut for Christmas decoration. Naturally, such cottages had productive gardens.

A characteristic cottage would be a simple thatched affair with lattice windows and a ladder inside leading to the upper storey. Outside there would be a porch with a bench or turf seat beside it, and a garden enclosed by a hedge or fence. The porch was always covered with climbers – honeysuckle, roses or everlasting pea – and there were masses of flowers. If the showiest were sunflowers, cabbage roses or hollyhocks, most of the flowers were either the traditional medicinal and scented herbs, sometimes planted in knots, or else the choicest of the wild-flowers which were varied and abundant in the neighbourhood. Let two quotations prove that in the 1820s, when Clare was writing these poems, the cottage garden was a reality:

Where rustic taste at leisure trimly weaves
The rose and straggling woodbine to the eaves,
And on the crowded spot that pales enclose
The white and scarlet daisy rears in rows,
Training the trailing peas in bunches neat,
Perfuming evening with a luscious sweet,
And sun-flowers planted for their gilded show,
That scale the window's lattice ere they blow.

And:

The timid maid,
Pleased to be praised, and yet of praise afraid,
Seeks the best flowers; not those of wood and fields,
But such as every farmer's garden yields –
Fine cabbage-roses, painted like her face,
The shining pansy, trimm'd with golden lace,
The tall-topped larkheels, feather'd thick with flowers,
The woodbine, climbing o'er the door in bowers,
The London tufts, of many a mottled hue,
The pale pink pea, and monkshood darkly blue,
The white and purple gilliflowers, that stay
Ling'ring, in blossom, summer half away,
The single blood-walls, of a luscious smell,
Old-fashion'd flowers which housewives love so well,
The columbines, stone-blue, or deep night-brown,
Their honeycomb-like blossoms hanging down
Each cottage-garden's fond adopted child,
Though heaths still claim them, where they yet grow wild.

One cottager, an old man, but active and literate, had a gardening book, none other than Thomas Tusser's *Hundred Good Points of Husbandry*, written in the sixteenth century. He possessed, in fact, five favourite books, the Bible, the prayer-book, *Pilgrim's Progress*, *The Death of Abel*, and 'prime old Tusser'.

His cottage is a place of humble rest
With one spare room to welcome every guest,
And that tall poplar pointing to the sky
His own hand planted when an idle boy,

44

> It shades his chimney while the singing wind
> Hums songs of shelter to his happy mind.

Perhaps no other writer has written quite so authentically from the very heart of cottage life as Clare, for he was the son of a labourer who was a pauper, and his first employment was the minding of sheep and geese on the common at his native Northamptonshire village, Helpstone. Though literary men tried to help him, he was always poor and later became insane, not a major poet, but a genuine cottager and countryman whose view of village life can be trusted.

In the Northern Counties

Prolific cottage gardening in the early nineteenth century was not confined to the south of England and the Midlands. Farmers, craftsmen and gentry in love with the rustic life were devoting themselves to gardening in Yorkshire and the Lake District, to which the romantic poets bear witness, some of whom were making gardens themselves.

Robert Southey, in his monumental prose work *The Doctor*, describes a yeoman's house and garden in the West Riding of Yorkshire:

> The house was to the east of the church, under the same hill, and with the same brook in front; and the intervening fields belonged to the family. It was a low house, having before it a little garden of that size and character which shewed that the inhabitants could afford to bestow a thought upon something more than mere bodily wants. You entered between two yew trees clipt to the fashion of two pawns. There were hollyhocks and sunflowers displaying themselves above the wall; roses and sweet peas under the windows, and the everlasting pea climbing the porch.
>
> The rest of the garden lay behind the house, partly on the slope of the hill. It had a hedge of gooseberry bushes, a few apple-trees, pot-herbs in abundance, onions, cabbages, turnips and carrots; potatoes had hardly yet found their way into these remote parts: and in a sheltered spot under the crag, open to the south, were six beehives which made the family perfectly independent of West Indian produce. Tea was in those days as little known as potatoes, and for all other things honey supplied the place of sugar.

I think that Southey was remembering this garden as it was at the turn of the nineteenth century. The yews clipped like pawns are interesting, for early references to cottage topiary are not very common; but cottagers undoubtedly practised this ancient craft, handed down from the Romans.

At exactly the same time the Wordsworths, William and his sister Dorothy, were making a garden at Dove Cottage, Grasmere. The best of Dorothy Wordsworth's literary work was her early journals, kept conscientiously in 1800 and 1802 (they lapsed in 1801). She was making a complete new garden with trees and shrubs, an orchard in meadow grass, and masses of flowers, vegetables and fruit, and there were beehives. Though the Wordsworths had paid help, William was diligent with the heavy work. Dorothy herself brought in many plants from the wild, set slips for hedges, sowed vegetables, hoed, weeded, sticked peas, pruned shrubs, obtained plants from a local vicar and from the farmers' wives, harvested vegetables and preserved fruit, especially gooseberries, and William dug, cut pea-sticks, raked stones from the soil, built seats and steps and a bower and cut down old trees. They seem to have been very good gardeners, and loved their flowers and produce as much as the abundant wild flowers and natural beauty of the Lake District where they took their celebrated rambles, alone, or with Coleridge, or with Mary Wordsworth after William's marriage. One day in June, 1800, Coleridge discovered a rock seat in the garden smothered in brambles which they began immediately to clear away.

From the countryside Dorothy brought in globe-flower (locally called lockety), strawberries, orchises, thyme, columbines, purple and white foxgloves, honeysuckle, snowdrops, buttercups and daisies; local friends gave them yellow and white lilies, sunflowers, bachelor's buttons (possibly a ranunculus, but many plants have been given this name), periwinkles, lemon-thyme and vegetable plants. They bought many shrubs from a local nurseryman.

The orchard was a favourite part of the Wordsworths' garden where, on a single day, they sowed scarlet beans, read *Henry V* aloud, and built a step. The orchard grass was full of wild flowers, and Dorothy recorded with delight the blooming of the primroses, celandines, violets, wood sorrel, stitchwort, foxgloves and vetches.

The Wordsworths and Coleridge not only brought in plants from the woods, but liked to sow garden flowers in the parks and woodlands to the possible confusion, Dorothy rightly comments, of future botanists. It is nice to think that the words 'possibly a garden escape' which often occur in wild-flower books ought in some cases to read 'sown by romantic poets'. Coleridge had a scheme for naturalizing laburnum in the Westmorland woods.

It is clear from Dorothy's journals that at Dove Cottage the two streams of gardening met. The garden was both romantic and useful, and in making it the Wordsworths drew on quite humble sources, collecting wild plants and accepting generous presents of plants from the farmers and cottagers round about.

4
Twenty Rods of Land

The poetic little gardens of Hampshire, Helpstone and the Lakes were not, unfortunately, typical of cottage gardens throughout the country. Cobbett praised some of the cottages of Kent, Sussex, Surrey and Hampshire, 'with a pig at almost every labourer's house' and 'some of the best gardens that I have seen in England', and William Howitt, a penetrating observer, recorded that between Dover and London he saw 'a hundred little spots I coveted with quite a heart-ache'; he also found charming gardens in Nottingham and Derbyshire, and pockets of contentment in Scotland, where he thought the cottagers better educated and less cloddish than in the south. But there is overwhelming evidence that most cottagers were ignorant and slovenly, their houses filthy and dilapidated, their gardens, if they had any land at all, ugly and neglected.

Fortunately, an army of radical reformers came on the scene in the first quarter of the nineteenth century demanding land for the rural poor, and the most successful of the crusaders was John Claudius Loudon. Pouring out books and articles on every conceivable aspect of gardening, high and low, he reached the most important audience – the landowners – and planted in the minds of many country gentlemen the novel idea that they ought to do something about their wretched tenants. In 1826, he started *The Gardener's Magazine*, a splendid journal which ran for seventeen years, ranging over the whole world of gardening from the parterres of Versailles to the cottager's pot of marigolds. Loudon is most often associated with the new villas which were springing up in the suburbs of our cities, and with their often princely pleasure gardens (which are not our subject), but he was just as deeply involved with cottage improvement.

An early contributor to the magazine was an excellent gentleman called J. H. Moggridge, Esq., a landowner, coal-owner and magistrate in Monmouthshire, who had built a village for his colliers in 1821, with an inn, a village hall, houses for the baker, blacksmith, tailor and shopkeepers, and cottages for the colliery workers. Each cottager was allotted 20 perches, or rods, of land, which is one-eighth of an acre. He decided to teach them gardening.

Progress was slow at first and some cottagers were curmudgeonly. 'The old cottager was well contented with a few square yards, sufficient to contain a few leeks and onions,' and many resisted his improvements. But he gave them cabbage plants from his own nursery, distributed apple-trees and gooseberry bushes, and introduced rhubarb. Quite soon, with only one exception, all the villagers' gardens were well cultivated, 'some of them highly, – producing peas, beans, potatoes, cabbages, cauliflowers, in the vegetable line and, more sparingly, some strawberries, and apples, in the fruit line. One poor fellow brought me, with great pride, his crop of apples from a French

Satisfaction from a well-managed plot.

Technical hints from J. C. Loudon: training trees.

graft.' Mr Moggridge also announced a scheme of competitions for the best cottage gardens and the best cottage produce, a shrewd move, for surely there is no department of life where prizes, cups and certificates have proved so strong a spur to effort as in gardening.

In later reports, Mr Moggridge announced even greater success. The cottagers were growing currants, gooseberries, strawberries, apples, rhubarb for tarts, and 'though more rarely, single plants and beds of flowers', and by 1832 one cottager was growing peaches and selling them for 8d. a dozen. Fifteen years earlier, in 1817, this man's garden had been a wilderness, and Mr Moggridge had cleared it at his own expense, to the fury of the neighbouring landlords. This cottager was a 'rough out-of-door carpenter, fence-mender and so on, who lived in a hovel with his wife and family'. Given some initial help, the man built himself a good house and two others for letting, his sons and daughters helped in the garden, there were many sorts of fruit and vegetables, honey from his own beehive, and a pig to kill at Christmas. But, unfortunately, the scheme in general suffered in 1832 from an industrial depression which was hitting Mr Moggridge himself.

Other landlords, some influenced by Loudon, others of their own volition, were making similar experiments. A Lord Cawdor in Pembrokeshire began a scheme of cottage improvements, the cottages to have small forecourts for flowers and larger gardens behind for produce. His head gardener reported:

I furnished them with such fruit-trees as were best adapted for the climate, and stocked their courts with herbaceous plants, shrubs, creepers of the common kinds, informing the cottagers at the same time that they would have to keep the whole in good order for the future; and I must observe that the information was not received with a good grace by some of them, prejudiced as they were against the introduction of anything new.

Again, the offer of prizes turned the tide, and 'the spirit of gardening soon became general and cuttings and seeds were in great demand'. Visitors came to see the gardens and 'gardeners who had never asked the name of a plant began to learn'.

Another landlord, in Wiltshire, planned a sensible scheme for cottages of different sizes to suit different family needs, each to have a good garden and a pigsty. A scheme of prizes for cottagers' cabbages, potatoes, carrots and nosegays was started in Somersetshire. By 1836 cottagers' societies were springing up all over Britain, and the older horticultural societies were opening sections for cottagers' exhibits. In some villages there were also prizes for bee-keeping and honey. One squire made a point of giving cottagers choice flowers of his own growing as well as common plants, but his offer of a change of vegetables was rejected, like John Evelyn's offer of free potatoes two centuries earlier. He gave one labourer some spare beetroot, but the family did not like it. 'Then, of course, you gave it to the pig?' 'Oh no, I was afraid it might do him harm.' An offer of spinach was equally unwelcome.

Some less practical landlords designed new cottage gardens under the whimsical influence of the Picturesque. A Mr Gregory built a model village at Harlaxton, Lincolnshire, with some useful two-storey cottages with ample gardens, set well back from the street, where every garden was 'laid out and planted by Mr Gregory's head gardener, creepers and climbers being introduced in proper places in such a manner as that no two gardens are planted with the same climbers'. Each garden had its own ornamented well, some with carpentry roofs, others with stone cupolas, no two alike, and each had its own boundary-line on the street, no two the same; some boundaries were walls of brick, others of stone, others again were hedged with holly, box, laurel or quickthorn. Inside the gardens were topiary, arbours, beehives, box-edged paths, flowering shrubs and fruit-trees. The total effect must have been fussy, a model village Sir Uvedale Price would have approved of; yet it must have been a pleasant place to live in. Possibly the squire's patronage was a little overwhelming, and the cottagers might have preferred to choose their own plants, but at least they were comfortable and received encouragement.

In all this movement towards better cottage gardening, the landlord's head gardener was an important person. Sometimes he acted under instructions, but often the gifts of seeds and cuttings depended largely on his goodwill, and sometimes the head gardener, not the squire, was the initiator of a scheme for improvement.

The progress of the cottager and his garden was highly regional, and patchy even within each region – in total, the bad cottages far outnumbered the good ones. Though many observers reported a tolerable standard as far north as Lancashire, and again in Scotland – William Howitt noted that the Scots farm-worker was well-educated, used book societies, and was well up in both local and national affairs – the counties between, especially Northumberland, seem to have been disastrously neglected, with absentee landlords and big farmers who shamelessly exploited their men. Often the cottagers shared their one-room hovels with the cow. But wherever there was a landlord interested in rural development, cottage gardens with flowers, veg-etables, fruit and livestock came into being. The difference between the good and bad landlord is nowhere better illustrated than in Disraeli's novel *Sybil: or, The Two Nations* (1845). The brutal Lord Marney, a nobleman with vast estates in the north country, is determined to reduce his responsibilities. 'I have taken care that the population of my parishes is not increased. I build no cottages, and I destroy all I can.' But the humanitarian mill-owner near by, Mr Trafford, builds a model village near the mill with gardens to every cottage and a well in every street, and encourages his men to buy their leases. There is a horticultural society in the village which holds annual competitions. He builds other cottages in the country where cottage craftsmen can still work at home.

> The cottage was recently built, and in a pleasing style ... A scarlet creeper clustered round one side of its ample porch; the windows were

large, mullioned, and neatly latticed; it stood in the midst of a garden of no mean dimensions, but every bed and nook of which teemed with cultivation; flowers and vegetables abounded, while an orchard rich with the promise of many fruits – ripe pears and famous pippins of the north and plums of every shape and hue – screened the dwelling from the wind.

The Ideal Plot and Its Yield

Opinions varied as to the ideal size for the cottager's plot. It will be remembered that Britton Abbot, the retired farm labourer with a fruitful garden near Tadcaster, Yorkshire, enclosed by a stalwart quickthorn hedge, had made it on a rood (quarter of an acre) of land leased to him by the squire. Both Abbot and the gentleman who based a pamphlet on his achievement in 1797 thought this the right size if a man was to feed his family well. In 1832, some authorities, urging landlords to build more substantial cottages, proposed as much as an acre, which would allow for two pigs a year. But others thought this far too much for a man who was already working hard on the land.

John Claudius Loudon himself usually took 20 rods,* or an eighth of an acre, as the ideal unit, enough, with a pig, fowls and ducks, to feed a

Carrot and cabbage, cottage staples for centuries.

* Not to be confused with a rood. A rood was a quarter of an acre, and 40 square rods, sometimes called perches, made a rood.

family of five, and he proposed that it should be cropped as follows:

1 rod onions and leeks
$\frac{1}{2}$ rod carrots
$\frac{1}{2}$ rod windsor beans
1 rod parsnips
3 rods cabbages, with a row of scarlet runners to be
   planted round the edges, to give a yield of 525 cabbages
4 rods early potatoes
4 rods Prussian potatoes
6 rods Devonshire potatoes

As an experiment, there might also be a handful of 'Cobbett's dwarf Indian corn', but planted more thickly than Cobbett himself recommended. This would, according to Loudon, provide some good feed for fowls and pigs, while the vegetables listed above would provide enough to feed the pig as well as the family.

Loudon said that some people might think the potato allowance small, but that in his opinion plenty of bacon, cabbage, carrots and good bread were all better than a mass of potatoes. One might note at this point that Cobbett was notoriously hostile to the potato, 'Ireland's lazy root', a typical Cobbett eccentricity. The Irish famine which was to follow proved only that exclusive reliance on the potato was reckless, not that the potato was a bad vegetable.

If space allowed, Loudon suggested radishes, early peas and beans, cos lettuce, barley, leeks and cucumber as possible extras. He also thought that the cottager might grow his own tobacco.

His plan for a 20-rod cottage garden omitted standard fruit-trees, for he thought that the cottager would save valuable space by training his currants, gooseberries, cherries, apples and pears against the house. He also suggested that the cottager should make use of wild food and bring in hop-roots from the hedges, for their tops were as tender as asparagus,* and should use fruiting hedges for his boundaries, especially sloes for wine or brandy. As a practical economy which

---

* I have tried this and Loudon was, as usual, right – cooked in salted water for two minutes, the shoots look and taste like thin sprue. Cobbett also liked hop-shoots and in *The English Garden* (1829) said they should be tied in bundles and boiled for half an hour, too long in my opinion.

would also provide shelter for the garden, he proposed high hedges of wildings grafted with good fruit – a hedge of wild crab-apple grafted with good apples, or pears grafted on wild pear, plums on wild sloe, cherries on wild gean. I have never myself seen this practice carried out in England, but it sounds eminently sensible. The hedges would not, of course, be clipped, but allowed to grow tall and pruned as necessary.

He also allowed for flowers, ornamental shrubs and climbers. This most practical and authoritative of gardeners said that 'the cultivation of a few Brompton or tenweek stocks, carnations, picotees, pinks and other flowers ought never to be omitted: they are the means of pure and constant gratification which Providence has afforded alike to the rich and the poor'. He added that these flowers, and prize gooseberries, were prime sources of amusement to weavers and mechanics.

Always ready to tell other people what they should do, he said that the hoeing, weeding and gathering of the garden were tasks for the gardener's wife and children, who might take on rabbits as well as the care of a pig, poultry, pigeons and a cat. Domestic rabbits had not yet made many appearances in the literature of the cottage garden, though William Salisbury, in a book called *The Cottager's Companion*, published in 1822, said that tame rabbits would pay the cottager well, adding naïvely 'the fecundity of the rabbit is beyond expectation'.

The Cottage Gardener, a magazine started rather later, in 1849, by George W. Johnson, 'for the amateur of moderate income and the cottager', or anyone with space for 'a bed of cabbages, a row of currant-trees and a flower border', gave a different cropping plan for the space of one-eighth of an acre, including one or two different vegetables. In good soil, the land should yield every year thirty bushels of potatoes, five of parsnips, five of carrots, five of beetroot, five of onions, 300 cabbages, some sprouts, many boilings of peas and beans, radishes and savoury herbs.

All the pundits of cottage gardening stressed the importance of good manure, and the cottager must save every scrap of useful material. First, of course, there was the pig's dung, then the slops and night-soil from the house and privy, then the garden refuse, such as vegetable stalks, weeds and grass mowings, then ashes and chimney soot, and then the scrapings of the roads and ditches, which the children must collect in bucket or handcart. All this potentially rich material was to be sunk in a pit and puddled near the privy, or made into a heap, mixed and turned regularly, to rot into manure within a year.

The privy had from time immemorial been an important source of soil fertility. By the mid nineteenth century human urine and excrement had been subjected to scientific analysis. *The Cottage Gardener* published the fascinating fact that 'the annual urine of two men is said to contain sufficient mineral food for an acre of land, and mixed with ashes will produce a fair crop of turnips'. When the shed at the bottom of the garden was supplanted by indoor plumbing the cottage garden was the poorer. I myself often stayed as a child in a cottage with an outdoor privy where squares cut from the *Daily Mail* and a bucket of ashes were placed beside the seat. All was used on the garden which grew, I remember, spectacularly good runner beans.

Victorian Patronage

The Cottage Gardener soon ceased to live up to its name and abandoned its early intention of catering for the small-time gardener, and switched to such subjects as stoves, orchids and other luxuries. (In 1861 it changed its name to the *Journal of Horticulture*.) Its standard never approached that of Loudon's *Gardener's Magazine*, either in scope or literary quality. Moreover, it fell into the fatal Victorian habit of moralizing, and where Loudon had been informative, Johnson was edifying.

I am afraid that by the middle of Queen Victoria's reign, the cottager was increasingly the victim of prosperous people who wished not so much to raise his standard of living as to improve his morals and, by keeping him busy in the garden, to keep him away from the demon drink. Women with not enough to do were particularly culpable, using cottage improvement as a boost to their own egos. There are two exquisite examples in Victorian novels of gentlewomen looking unctuously for something to improve.

Miss Marjoribanks, in Mrs Oliphant's delightful novel of that name, published in 1865, was longing to get her hands on a village called Marchbank, where she was going to start her married life.

7. The gooseberry was a favourite nineteenth-century fruit.
The variety Compton's Sheba's Queen was painted by Mrs A. I. Withers in 1825
for *Drawings of Fruit*, by William Hooker *et al*.

Pl. 88

8. Polyanthus and auriculas were among the original eight accepted florists' flowers.
In this plate from Jane Loudon's *The Ladies' Flower Garden of Ornamental Perennials* (1841)
are a polyanthus called Burnard's Formosa, a green paste-centred auricula, The Conqueror
of Europe (note the circular form) and double varieties of the common primrose.

1 Fritillaria imperialis 2 Fritillaria Persica B. 3 Fritillaria Persica 4 Fritillaria leucocantha.
5 Fritillaria meleagris 6 Fritillaria Pyrenaica 7 Fritillaria lutea 8 Fritillaria obliqua

9. Fritillaria imperialis, or crown imperial, was an early cottage-garden flower.
Other fritillaries in this plate from Jane Loudon's *The Ladies' Flower*
Garden of Ornamental Bulbous Plants are *F. persica* (two forms), *F. leucocantha,*
F. meleagris, F. pyrenaica, F. lutea and *F. obliqua.*

Pl.50.

1 *Tulipa oculus solis.* 2 *Tulipa cornuta.* 3 *Tulipa sylvestris.* 4 *Tulipa Clusiana.*
5 *Tulipa suaveolens.* 6 *Tulipa montana.* 7 *Tulipa Capensis.* 8 *Tulipa biflora.*

10. *Tulipa* species recommended by Jane Loudon included *T. oculus-solis, T. cornuta,*
T. sylvestris, T. clusiana, T. suaveolens, T. montana, T. capensis and *T. biflora.*

There was a village not far from the gates at Marchbank, where every kind of village nuisance was to be found. There are people who are very tragical about village nuisances, and there are other people who assail them with loathing, as a duty forced upon their consciences; but Lucilla was neither of the one way of thinking nor the other. It gave her the liveliest satisfaction to think of all the disorder and disarray of the Marchbank village. Her fingers itched to be at it – to set all the crooked things straight, and clean away the rubbish, and set everything, as she said, on a sound foundation. If it had been a model village, with prize flower-gardens and clean as Arcadia, the thought of it would not have given Miss Marjoribanks half so much pleasure. The recollection of all the wretched hovels and miserable cottages exhilarated her heart.

Mrs Oliphant saw her self-satisfied heroine with ironical eyes. George Eliot thought of Dorothea Brooke, heroine of *Middlemarch* (1871–2) as a noble character, but Dorothea suffered from the same irritating wish to improve the lot of others for her own gratification. She was about to marry an elderly, well-to-do parson in the village of Lowick.

Everybody, he assured her, was well off in Lowick: not a cottager in those double cottages at a low rent but kept a pig, and the strips of garden at the back were well tended. . . . The speckled fowls were so numerous that Mr Brooke observed, 'Your farmers leave some barley for the women to glean, I see.'

Dorothea sank into silence on the way back to the house. She felt some disappointment, of which she was yet ashamed, that there was nothing for her to do in Lowick; and in the next few minutes her mind had glanced over the possibility, which she would have preferred, of finding that her home would be in a parish which had a larger share of the world's misery.

Turning from fiction to fact, an official report in the 1860s commented, 'On entering an improved cottage, with a neat and civilized garden, in which the leisure hours of the husband are pleasantly and profitably employed, it will be found that he has no desire to frequent the beershop, or spend his evenings away from home, the children are reared to labour, to habits and feelings of independence, and taught to connect happiness with industry, and to shrink from idleness and immorality; the girls make good servants,

Model cottages near Derby.

obtain the confidence of their employers, and are promoted to the best situations.' All very true, but rather cold-blooded.

However, even if the Victorian attitude was patronizing, the results were a wonderful improvement in the cottager's standard of living, and there were now many more good cottagers' gardens than there had been in 1800. One commentator has claimed that 'estate cottages are, perhaps, the most enduring memorial of the Victorian social order'.[*]

The new or improved cottages were built with various aims in mind. There were, as there had been for more than a century, enlightened squires who built model cottages for their labourers, but the standard was now higher, with a norm of two or three bedrooms. There were also a few rich people, not necessarily landowners, who built as a matter of social conscience. More important numerically were the new tycoons, mill-owners, or mine-owners, or Quakers like the Cadburys, who built small cottage-towns near their factories. Some were embryo slums, with back-to-back houses and no land, but others were delightful, with

---

[*] 'The Myth of Cottage Life', by Nicholas Cooper, a series of two articles in *Country Life*, 1967.

well-planned terraced or semi-detached cottages with good gardens, and these gardens are certainly our concern, for a cottage is not necessarily rural. The tenants were usually better educated and better paid than the country cottagers, and some were keen members of the flower and produce societies.

Allotments and Allotment-Gardens

Another way of providing land for cottagers in the nineteenth century was the allotment – a strip of land not attached to the house. The first Act of Parliament permitting parishes to acquire land to provide strips of allotment was passed in 1819, and other Acts were passed at intervals. The allotment system did not enjoy instant success. In some counties, no allotments were provided at all, in others a certain number were provided and used, in others, again, the privately provided allotment, with the tenant paying rent to the landlord rather than the parish, was more popular than the official system.

What was enormously successful was the allotment-*garden*, sometimes provided just outside the towns for tradespeople or mechanics who may have had no land in the town at all, but could afford a substantial rent. These were larger than mere strips, often a quarter of an acre or more in extent, and the whole family would make a trip to them on leisure days, with picnic baskets and toys for the children, much as we would use a weekend caravan. They were pleasure gardens as well as gardens for produce, and had summer-houses and seats, and perhaps a rockery or fernery, a grass plot for the children, and vegetables, flowers and fruit. As early as 1838, Howitt had commented on the many allotment-gardens on the outskirts of Nottingham. There were more than 5,000 of them, about a quarter of an acre in size, rented by mechanics.

> In the winter, they have rather a desolate aspect, with their naked trees and hedges, and all their little summer-houses exposed, damp-looking and forlorn; but in spring and summer they look exceedingly well, – in spring, all starred with blossoms, all thick with leaves; and their summer-houses peeping pleasantly from among them. The advantage of these gardens to the working-class of a manufacturing town is beyond calculation. . . .

Early in spring, they get into their gardens, tidy, clear and dig. Trees are pruned, beds are dug, walks cleaned, and all the refuse and decayed vegetables piled up in heaps. . . .

Every garden has its summer-house; and these are of all scales and grades, from the erection of a few tub-staves, with an attempt to train a pumpkin or a wild-hop over it, to substantial brick-houses with glass windows, good cellars for a deposit of choice wines, a kitchen and all necessary apparatus, and a good pump to supply them with water. Many are very picturesque rustic huts, built with great taste, and hidden by tall hedges in a perfect little paradise of lawn and shrubbery.

These, clearly, are the gardens of substantial tradespeople, but even the operatives, who may not have run to the 'choice wines', made their allotment-gardens attractive. 'Many of the mechanics have very excellent summer-houses, and there they delight to go, and smoke a solitary pipe with a friend, or to spend a Sunday afternoon, or a summer evening, with their families.'

Howitt says that no other town had so many of these gardens on the outskirts as Nottingham.

The Turn of the Tide

By the middle of Queen Victoria's reign, or let us say by 1860, cottage gardens were more numerous, more varied in kind, and more richly planted than ever before. (One must always make the proviso that cottage life crumbled where there was a bad landlord.)

One might fairly take 1860 as the zenith of the old cottage garden, for in the second half of the century it slowly changed its nature. Of course thousands of the old gardens went on as before, but many did not. First, the florists' societies began a slow decline, as the cottage artisan became increasingly a factory mechanic and worked long hours in a mill, instead of at home – the sooty pollution of the industrial towns was an added discouragement. Secondly, there was an agricultural depression on the way, and in the 1880s many small farmers went bankrupt and many labourers were destitute and drifted to the towns. Thirdly, the bedding craze affected quite a number of cottage gardeners (see Chapter 8). And fourthly – a more subtle change – cottage gardening lost some of its spontaneity and became a cult. Artists, writers and photographers 'discovered' cottage gardening like some charming antique, and though cottagers in remote districts went on making simple, useful gardens as of old, the newer gardens were often larger and more sophisticated, with an increasing number of foreign and tender plants.

Cottage gardening had become an art form. It is still one of the dominating influences in gardening today.

5
Authentic Cottage
Plants and Cooking

We all talk loosely about 'cottage plants', meaning just about everything we have seen in a sentimental Christmas card or calendar, with impossibly bright herbaceous borders leading to a timbered cottage smothered with roses and wisteria. But some of the flowers in the Christmas card are not old cottage plants at all – the multi-coloured lupins and the hybrid tea-roses are not old and the wisteria is not very cottagey. One must try to find criteria by which to judge what are true cottage plants, rather than plants grown by everyone from the landed gentry to the rat-catcher.

Much of the old gardening literature was written for rich men with squads of gardeners and is not useful to us here; nor are the early nurserymen's lists, such as those of London and Wise, who were supplying plants to mansions like Chatsworth and Blenheim. It is not antiquity alone which makes a cottage plant. We have grown oranges in England for more than 300 years, but who would associate them with a cottage?

I count as cottage plants:

1. Useful wild plants which would cost the poor man nothing to acquire and which he certainly transplanted from woods and fields. We have evidence of herbs within the cottage yard as early as Chaucer.

2. Plants, whether useful or decorative, recommended by the early pundits like Thomas Tusser and John Worlidge for the garden of the husbandman and his wife.

3. Plants which have for centuries provided cheap food for the poor.
4. Plants loved by bees.
5. Plants regarded as old cottage specialities by the cottage-conscious writers of the nineteenth century. Some, like Miss Mitford and John Clare, wrote from personal experience, later writers like Miss Jekyll were scholars of the subject.
6. Plants recommended for cottagers by publicists like John Claudius Loudon and George W. Johnson, who took up the cottager's cause.
7. Florists' flowers.

Many of these plant names have to be winkled out of non-specialist literature, including fiction, not without difficulty. The choice of 1860 as a turning-point is somewhat arbitrary, for, of course, cottage

Single and double violets were not only pretty, but useful.

gardening has never stopped. But in talking of 'authentic cottage plants' one has to put a deadline somewhere, and I feel that plants introduced after 1860, though they may fit worthily into a modern cottage garden, are not part of the old picture. Since long plant lists make heavy reading I have relegated my lists, taken from selected source of different dates, to the Appendix on page 145. I venture here a few personal reflections on the old plants.

Old Cottage Plants

Plants Earned Their Keep. The early garden plants were much more fully used than are plants today. Most herbs, whether grown in the garden or gathered wild, were neither purely medicinal nor purely culinary, but were used for all sorts of purposes, flowers, leaves, roots, seeds, all being called upon as needed. For instance, the humble violet, which to us is a posy flower, was an important plant in the Middle Ages and for a long time afterwards, being woven into garlands, made into syrups, chopped into salads, stuffings and sauces, and strewn on the floor to discourage fleas. That pretty little weed, sweet woodruff, was used as a strewing plant, a stuffing for mattresses, a stimulating ingredient in wine and an antidote, when infused, for all sorts of complaints from headaches to consumption. Flowers in the garden worked their passage, and continued to do so until the middle of the nineteenth century when, gradually, chemistry overtook herbalism in the medical field, and cooks increasingly turned to shops rather than the garden for their ingredients.

Cottage Vegetables. I think it is clear from Thomas Tusser that the vegetable garden as we know it was established in Elizabethan times. Tusser's lists for the small farmer's garden are substantial (see Appendix) and most of his vegetables are confirmed by William Harrison in his *Description of England* and, a little later, by John Parkinson. Tusser's vegetable garden has asparagus, beans, beets, cabbage, carrots, cucumbers, globe artichokes, gourds, leeks, onions, parsnips, peas, pumpkins, radishes, skirret, spinach and turnips. The most important absentees are potatoes and tomatoes, which arrived later, and of course the old varieties of vegetables were less productive than modern ones. On the other hand, I suspect that Elizabethan farmhouse salads were a great deal better than the average cottage offering today, which usually consists of a bowl of unripe tomatoes. Tusser lists a wide range of salad herbs, like tarragon and sorrel, which would be mixed, perhaps, with cress, radishes and flowers, and dressed with salt and vinegar.

I do not for a moment suppose that many husbandmen grew all Tusser's vegetables; after all, few of us today grow more than a fraction of the vegetables in Sutton's *Seed Catalogue*. And sometimes Tusser's thoughts seem to stray from the small farmer and his wife to richer households, with money to buy imported luxuries like olives and lemons. But on the whole I find his picture of the cottage vegetable garden lively and convincing.

Bee Plants. Beekeeping is one of the oldest of the cottager's skills, and as soon as cottagers began to make order out of chaos and to plan their garden space and grow more than a few basic crops, I think that some would have grown plants rich in nectar for their bees. I cannot pretend to put a date on the first cottage bee garden, but would guess at the late sixteenth or early seventeenth century.

Planting for bees is not an economic proposition, but a labour of love. Bees forage for half a mile or more from their hives and would get only a negligible supply of food from a patch of clover or hyssop in the garden. But most beekeepers love their bees and like to watch them working and it would be natural to plant a sunny area with the herbs and flowers which are richest in nectar and pollen. In the early days these would have been native plants, particularly mignonette, borage, scabious, poppies, thyme and most of the labiate herbs, and also lavender; and in later centuries, when we know that keen apiarists cultivated bee gardens, there would be many new flowers and flowering shrubs – one famous bee plant is *Limnanthes douglasii*, introduced from North America in 1833. Bees prefer to work on a large patch of one plant rather than a mixture, and they do not work double flowers.

Even cottagers with no sentiment for their bees and no wish to waste time on bee plants when wild flowers were plentiful might still have thought it worth while to plant June flowers to fill 'the June gap' – a period in early June between the spring fruit blossom and the sunburst of summer perennials, when bees may go short of nectar. Perhaps this idea that bee plants featured in quite early cottage gardens is too fanciful; but the bee garden was an established feature by 1800.

Quintessential Cottage Flowers. All the plants in this book are cottage plants, but some are more cottagey than others – either antiquity, or the love which cottagers have borne them, have earned them a special place. From the hundreds of flowers which qualify I have chosen ten as the embodiment of cottage gardening.

Lilium candidum is rightly called the Cottage Lily. Introduced into Britain from the eastern Mediterranean at a very early unknown date, it is one of the few non-native flowers recommended by Jon the Gardener (see Appendix). Tusser suggests it for windows and pots. It hates

1 *Caryophyllus maximus rubro varius*. The great old Carnation or gray Hulo. 2 *Caryophyllus maier rubro & albo varius*. The white Carnation. 3 *Caryophyllus albo rubens*. The Camberfine or the Poole flower. 4 *Caryophyllus Cantij striatus*. The faire made of Kent. 5 *Caryophyllus Sabaudicus carneus*. The blush Sanadge. 6 *Caryophyllus Xerampelinus*. The Gredeline Carnation. 7 *Caryophyllus disfans Grimæ's*. The Grimele or Primer. 8 *Caryophyllus albus maior*, The great white Gilloflower. 9 *Elegans Heroina Bradshawy*, Master Bradshawes dainty Lady.

disturbance, and the permanent planting of the cottage garden suits it well.

Gilliflowers, or clove-scented pinks, come next. Many kinds of dianthus were popular by Elizabethan times, including carnations and sweet williams, but none more so than clipping pinks. Parkinson grew twenty-nine different varieties, and John Rea in 1665 had three times as many. Pinks were among the ten accepted florists' flowers of the late eighteenth century and were beloved by the Victorians. I have heard various derivations of the word gilliflower, but the most convincing is that it means 'clove-scented', coming from *giroflier*, the French for a clove-tree.

Honeysuckle, or woodbine, is the oldest climber in the garden, planted by the door or in the arbour, rivalled only by the sweet briar, or eglantine. Pundits and poets alike have always associated it with cottages. Sir Uvedale Price valued its picturesque spirals on a cottage porch; John Clare wrote, 'Where rustic taste at leisure trimly weaves/The rose and straggling woodbine to the eaves.'

Mignonette is mentioned in early plant lists, but it was the Victorians who revelled in the plant. Scarcely any other flower is so often mentioned in Victorian literature. George W. Johnson, in his introduction to his new magazine, *The Cottage Gardener*, in 1849, says that his aim is to make 'the Cabbage more productive, the Apples more abundant, the Mignonette more enduring'. And there is a pleasant scene in Mrs Oliphant's *Miss Marjoribanks*, describing a row of cottages in a small country town.

> By this time it was getting dark, and it was very pleasant in Grove Street, where most of the good people had just watered their little gardens, and brought out the sweetness of the mignonette. Mr Cavendish was not sentimental, but still the hour was not without its influence; and when he looked at the lights that began to appear in the parlour windows, and breathed in the odours from the little gardens, it is not to be denied that he asked himself for a moment what was the good of going through all this bother and vexation, and whether love in a cottage, with a little garden full

(Opposite) Carnations and pinks, from Parkinson's *Paradisi*.

of mignonette and a tolerable amount of comfort within, was not, after all, a great deal more reasonable than it looked at first sight.

Primroses were used for cooking in the Middle Ages, and were a very early garden plant. In the seventeenth century country housewives greatly prized coloured primroses and double primroses, especially the hose-in-hose varieties which are rare treasures today. The old primroses, and also the even rarer hose-in-hose cowslips, were preserved in cottage gardens in the nineteenth century when perennials were banished from large gardens in favour of bedding plants.

Lavender was introduced into Britain from the Mediterranean and was well established by the Middle Ages. By Tusser's time it was a common strewing herb, and became increasingly popular with the Elizabethan fashion for clipped edgings. The best of all scented herbs for drying, and a famous bee plant, a lavender bush is a traditional feature by the cottage door.

Roses are a universal delight and a rose means as much to the palace as the cottage; but since no cottage flower garden has ever been made without a rose, it must be included. The early cottage roses were single wild roses, but by the time of the romantic poets, the cabbage rose was the cottage speciality. Miss Jekyll regarded double banksian roses (introduced 1824) and cluster roses like The Garland (1835) as traditional cottage plants.

The oriental hollyhock, *Althaea rosea*, came early to Britain, probably in 1573, but the marsh mallow, *Althaea officinalis*, was mentioned even before this by Jon the Gardener and Tusser. The foreign hollyhock soon became popular and the Rev. Samuel Gilbert in 1683 stigmatized double hollyhocks as rubbish adored by country-women, so this is a true cottage plant. Robert Southey loved it in a farmhouse garden and John Clare wrote: 'Here beside the modest stock/Flaunts the flaring hollyhock.' By 1840 it had become a florists' flower, and from 1850 it featured in every water-colour of a cottage scene.

Hawthorn, or quickthorn, is the oldest of English hedging plants and is still the most delightful, with its wonderfully fresh green leaves in spring. It was clipped into arbours from earliest times and has probably provided more country hedges than all other hedging plants put together. Jon the Gardener lists it and in 1797 Britton Abbot chose it for his model cottage garden at Tadcaster.

Amaranthus, Flower Gentle, or Prince's Feather, which is probably *A. hypochondriacus*, appears in Tusser as a flower for windows and pots, and in the following century both John Rea and John Worlidge call *Amaranthus caudatus*, or Love-lies-bleeding, a countrywoman's flower. Of course, John Clare has it: 'As lady's laces, everlasting peas,/True-love-lies-bleeding, with the heart's-at-ease.' *Amaranthus* is one of the very few cottage flowers I have never personally cared for.

I am aware how arbitrary this list must seem, with such cottage favourites as stocks, sweet peas, columbines, wallflowers, nigella, sweet rocket and marigolds omitted; there are many other contenders for a place. I will end with two surprising plants which are *not* authentic cottage plants. The editor of *The Cottage Gardener* reported in 1849 that he had never seen either *Cyclamen hederaefolium* or *C. coum* in a cottage garden; he would see them everywhere today.

From Garden to Kitchen

How did the cottage housewife use her garden for food? I am thinking here of the working-class cottager only, who had her own special problems, notably, lack of money, and her own ways of making ends meet. The cottage gentry and the rich farmers would have had no difficulty at any period in keeping an excellent table and there are many modern cookery books of delicious dishes based on traditional English country fare.

Cookery books specially written for poor people do not appear until after 1800, but there are passing references to 'food for the poor' in much older cookery books, herbals and general literature. Putting the old and the new together, I think we can assume that cottage cookery changed very little over hundreds of years.

By 1860 a number of books for the poor were in circulation, including *A Cookery Book for the Working Classes* (1852), by Charles Elmé Francatelli, 'late maître d'hotel and chief cook to H.M. the Queen', who took the subject seriously, and *Soyer's Shilling Cookery for the People* (early 1850s), by Alexis Soyer, the famous French chef of the

Farmhouse cooking was often on a generous scale.

Reform Club who went to the Crimea to improve the appalling food being served to the troops. Esther Copley's *The Complete Cottage Cookery* (*circa* 1840), was practical to the point of bleakness, for Mrs Copley was of Huguenot extraction and took a tiresome moral tone, suggesting that, if the poor gave up beer, tobacco, sweets and tea, they would have more to spend on proper nourishment.

The most important recipes in the Victorian cottage cookery books were for making bread and puddings; for using the pig; for making soup; and for cooking the small range of vegetables which the cottager was willing to grow. In ancient cottage cooking there were, of course, no potatoes, and the poor used honey instead of sugar for sweetening and preserving until well into the eighteenth century, but otherwise the ingredients were much the same in the nineteenth century as they had been for three or four hundred years.

Another important branch of cottage cookery from earliest times was the use of fruit, vegetables and herbs for wines and preserves. I can find few examples at any period of egg recipes for the poor (though eggs were lavishly used in sauces and puddings in rich households) and think the reason must be that when a pig has to be fed there is not much corn or meal available for poultry; hens which scratch about for their own food may be edible, if stringy, but they won't lay many eggs. On a big farm there would of course be all kinds of poultry, but the rich farmer in the Victorian age had risen so far above the small farmer and the labourer in status and wealth that he has classed himself out of this book.

I have confined the following notes to cottagers' specialities made from their own animal and vegetable garden produce. Though the recipes included were printed at the dates given, most of them would have been in circulation for a long time, handed down from mother to daughter.

Bread and Puddings. Bread was always the staple cottage food. In prosperous times the dough was made of wheat-flour mixed with fat, milk or water, salt, and sugar or treacle if available, leavened with yeast, but when economy was pressing the wheat-flour was mixed with rye-flour, barley-flour, or potato-flour. (At one dire period, as mentioned earlier, it was mixed with acorns.) Boiled suet puddings were an important item of diet, more economical than baked puddings as the flour expands more when boiled and makes a larger pudding. A boiled meat-and-onion pudding, with far more onions than meat, made in a basin lined with suet crust and covered with a cloth, was a well-known stand-by. Sweet boiled suet puddings filled with fruit were also popular. In the north of England, batter puddings, often strongly flavoured with herbs, were much used in farmhouses and cottages, as they are today.

The Pig. Recipes for using the cottage pig are abundant, from butchering and curing the beast to using its less attractive parts for soup. It must be remembered that often the family would be able to keep only half their annual pig for themselves, as the other half might have to be exchanged for essential groceries and spices – helpings of bacon were not handed round the family with a lavish hand. The following recipes show how every bit of the animal was used.

Bacon and Cabbage Soup (1852)

This is on the principle of a French *pot-au-feu*, when the soup is served first and the meat later. Hungry children stuffed with soup would not want so much bacon afterwards.

Put your piece of bacon on to boil in a pot with 2 gallons water, when it has been boiled up and been well skimmed, add cabbages, kale, greens or sprouts, whichever may be used, well washed and split down, and also some parsnips and carrots; season with pepper, but no salt as the bacon will be salty. Boil very gently for two hours, take out the bacon, cabbage, parsnips and carrots, leaving a few vegetables in the soup, and pour this into a large bowl containing slices of bread. Eat the soup first, and bacon later.

A Bacon Salad (1852)

Make a salad with whatever you have, corn salad, lettuce, mustard-and-cress, beetroot, onion, etc., cut up into a bowl. Cut some fat bacon into small square pieces, fry, pour at once upon the salad. Add vinegar, salt and pepper to taste.

Pig's Fry (1852)

This consists of the pig's heart, liver, lights and some of the chitterlings; these are to be first cut up in slices, then seasoned with pepper and salt, rolled in a little flour, and fried with some kind of grease in the frying-pan. As the pieces are fried, place them on their dish to keep hot before the fire, and when all is done, throw some chopped onions and sage leaves into the pan, to be fried of a light colour. Add a very little flour, pepper and salt, a gill of water and a few drops of vinegar. Boil up this gravy and pour it over the pig's fry.

Other well-liked pig dishes were brawn, made with the head, hocks and feet of the pig, and broad beans with parsley sauce and as much bacon as could be spared, cooked with cloves and a little brown sugar. Lard made from the pig was usually flavoured with sprigs of rosemary, and rosemary lard spread on bread might be a main meal when other food was scarce.

Soups. Soup or pottage had been a staple cottage dish – sometimes, the only hot cottage dish, with the possible exception of toasted cheese – from time immemorial. The soup was of vegetables, herbs, chopped bones or scraps of meat if possible, and seasoning, poured over slices of bread. If vegetables were plentiful, the pottage was sometimes made into a purée and called a 'porridge'.

A more enterprising soup, called pease soup, was made from the boiled feet, hocks and ears of a pig, with peas, onions or leeks, celery, carrots, parsnips, turnips, parsley, mint and seasoning. Sometimes soups were thickened with oatmeal, especially in the north of Britain.

Vegetables. I do not think one can pretend that the cottager ever did anything subtle in the way of vegetable cookery. Alexis Soyer in the early 1850s deplored the low standard of vegetable cooking throughout England, but especially in country districts. Vegetables were mostly used for soup, or for boiling with any kind of meat, particularly bacon. They were not cooked separately from the meat, but were put in a cloth and added to the pot about half-an-hour before the meat was done. A favourite recipe was for a piece of bacon boiled with brown sugar and cloves, with broad beans in a cloth added later.

Lettuces, radishes and other salads were popular at a surprisingly early date – certainly in Elizabethan times – and were eaten with bread or bread-and-butter. The most interesting vegetable dish I have been able to find is stuffed onions, of which there are many variants; the onions were stuffed with meat stuffings if available, otherwise with bread-and-herb stuffings, and were either boiled or baked. Peas and broad beans were dried in a plentiful summer, so that there would be a change from cabbage and leeks in winter.

Herbs. The cottage housewife was much more skilled with herbs than with vegetables, for the herbal tradition is as old as English history. She grew the herbs she liked and used them fresh, and dried them in the wind or in a draught indoors for winter use. She used them to flavour dishes just as we do today, but she had one accomplishment which is almost lost. She made many herb teas, which were drunk for refreshment, as an economy, or as a medicine. Esther Copley suggests strawberry-leaf tea; hawthorn-leaf tea, picked and dried with leaves of balm and sage; and a tea made of equal parts of agrimony, balm, tormentil and wild marjoram with a few leaves of roses, black currants and cowslip flowers.

Another Victorian writer recommends hop teas for digestion, dandelion tea infused with sugar or honey for bilious affections, lime-flower tea for hysteria, hyssop tea for worms, balm and borage tea for

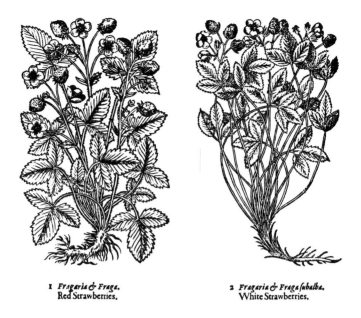

1 *Fragaria & Fraga.*
Red Strawberries.

2 *Fragaria & Fraga subalba.*
White Strawberries.

cooling an over-heated system. These, he points out, are all very cheap, and most do not need sweetening. Here is one characteristic recipe:

Strawberry-leaf Tea (1840)

Gather the leaves while young and tender, pick off the stalks, and dry them in an airy but shady place; when a sufficient quantity is collected, and the whole is perfectly dry, it may be kept in a canister or bottle, as other teas, and used in the same manner.

Wines, Jams, Jellies and Pickles. All these were made from both garden and wild fruits and vegetables wherever the cottage housewife could afford the necessary sugar, spices and other bought ingredients. Parsnip, dandelion and elderflower and (melancholy thought) cowslip wines, red currant, gooseberry and blackberry jellies, pickled damsons and pears, rhubarb jam and quince cheese would be made in all but the poorest kitchens, for use on special occasions. The old art of preserving reached a peak in the nineteenth century, and most of the recipes we use today have been handed down from our grandmothers and great-grandmothers, with just enough adaptation to suit modern cookers and utensils; they can be found in many modern cookery books and it would be superfluous to repeat them here. However, one product of the old gardens, mead, is rare in the modern cellar and deserves a little space. Once drunk by all classes of society, it had lost caste by Victorian times except in the villages, where it was still made by cottagers who kept bees.

To begin with, there is mead and mead, and Sir Kenelm Digby, the philosopher, scientist and general political trouble-maker who died in 1665, collected no fewer than fifty-six different recipes from friends, and his collection was published four years later. Mead is a fermented honey drink, and as honey will ferment of itself, mead may be made with or without added yeast, the latter method being generally held to be superior. Variants included sack mead, with sack and brandy added, metheglin, with spices or herbs added, cowslip mead and walnut mead. Here are two recipes, one of Sir Kenelm Digby's in 1669 and one published in *The Female Economist,* by Mrs Smith, in 1810.

Mead with Yeast (1669)

Take 1 measure of honey to 3 of water, boil gently until one-third is boiled away. Take a *garni* of violet leaves, strawberry leaves, sorrell, rosemary, balm, hart's tongue, liverwort, thyme and red sage. Simmer the honey again for 1 hour. Remove the *garni* and add cloves, nutmeg and ginger. Add some Blue Raisins of the Sun and some yeast, cover with a thick cloth during fermentation, and when finished strain it into a storage jar until it clears, then bottle and mature for two years.

Mead Wine (1810)

Take 1 gallon of water to 4 to 5 lb honey, 2 oz of hops to every 10 gallons the above, the rinds of 3 to 4 lemons, a few coriander seeds. Put the water on to heat and when it is hot add the honey and bring to the boil, removing the scum as it rises. Boil for 1½ hours. Add the lemon rinds and coriander seeds, sewn into a bag. Remove from the heat. When cold, put into a cask, stop it tight, and let it stand for 9 to 12 months. Then draw off the wine and bottle.

There is a delightful episode in George Borrow's picaresque story *Romany Rye* (1857) in which he drinks a cup of mead for the first time and finds it highly intoxicating.

Borrow has come upon an old man weeping by the roadside because his ass has been stolen from him by a confidence trickster. Borrow pursues the rogue and brings back the ass, and the old man invites him to his cottage to taste his mead.

As I had never tasted mead, of which I had frequently read in the compositions of the Welsh bards, and, moreover, felt rather thirsty from the heat of the day, I told him that I should have great pleasure in attending him. Whereupon, turning off together, we proceeded about half a mile, sometimes between stone walls, and at other times hedges, till we reached a small hamlet, through which we passed, and presently came to a very pretty cottage, delightfully situated within a garden, surrounded by a hedge of woodbines. Opening a gate at one corner of the garden, he led the way to a large shed, which stood partly behind the cottage, which he said was his stable; thereupon he dismounted and led his donkey, after taking off her caparisons, and I followed his example, tying my horse at the other side with a rope halter which he gave me; he then asked me to come in and taste his mead, but I told him that I must attend to the comfort of my horse first, and forthwith, taking a wisp of straw, rubbed him carefully down. Then taking a pailful of clear water which stood in the shed, I allowed the horse to drink about half a pint; and then turning to the old man, who all the time had stood by looking at my proceedings, I asked him whether he had any oats? 'I have all kinds of grain,' he replied; and, going out, he presently returned with two measures, one a large and the other a small one, both filled with oats, mixed with a few beans, and handing the large one to me for the horse, he emptied the other before the donkey, who, before she began to dispatch it, turned her nose to her master's face, and fairly kissed him. Having given my horse his portion, I told the old man that I was ready to taste his mead as soon as he pleased, whereupon he ushered me into his cottage, where, making me sit down by a deal table in a neatly sanded kitchen, he produced from an old-fashioned closet a bottle, holding about a quart, and a couple of cups, which might each contain about half a pint, then opening the bottle and filling the cups with a brown-coloured liquor, he handed one to me, and taking a seat opposite to me, he lifted the other, nodded, and saying to me, 'Health and welcome,' placed it to his lips and drank.

'Health and thanks,' I replied; and being very thirsty, emptied my cup at a draught; I had scarcely done so, however, when I half repented. The mead was deliciously sweet and mellow, but appeared strong as brandy; my eyes reeled in my head, and my brain became slightly dizzy. 'Mead is a strong drink,' said the old man, as he looked at me, with a half smile on his countenance. 'This is, at any rate,' said I, 'so strong indeed, that I would not drink another cup for any consideration.' 'And I would not ask you,' said the old man; 'for, if you did, you would most probably be stupid all day, and wake next morning with a headache. Mead is a good drink, but woundily strong, especially to those who be not used to it, as I suppose you are not.' 'Where do you get it?' said I. 'I make it myself,' said the old man, 'from the honey which my bees make.' 'Have you many bees?' I enquired. 'A great many,' said the old man. 'And do you keep them,' said I, 'for the sake of making mead with their honey?' 'I keep them', he replied, 'partly because I am fond of them, and partly for what they bring me in; they make me a great deal of honey, some of which I sell, and with a little I make me some mead to warm my poor heart with, or occasionally to treat a friend with like yourself.' 'And do you support yourself entirely by means of your bees?' 'No,' said the old man; 'I have a little bit of ground behind my house, which is my principal means of support.' 'And do you live alone?' 'Yes,' said he; 'with the exception of the bees and the donkey, I live quite alone.' 'And have you always lived alone?' The old man emptied his cup, and his heart being warmed with the mead, he told me his history, which was simplicity itself. His father was a small yeoman, who, at his death, had left him, his only child, the cottage, with a small piece of ground behind it, and on this little property he had lived ever since. About the age of twenty-five he had married an industrious young woman, by whom he had one daughter, who died before reaching years of womanhood. His wife, however, had survived her daughter many years, and had been a great comfort to him, assisting him in his rural occupations; but, about four years before the present period, he had lost her, since which time he had lived alone, making himself as comfortable as he could; cultivating his ground, with the help of a lad from the neighbouring village, attending to his bees, and, occasionally riding his donkey to market, and hearing the word of God, which he said he was sorry he could not read, twice a week regularly at the parish church. Such was the old man's tale.

When he had finished speaking, he led me behind his house, and showed me his little domain. It consisted of about two acres in admirable cultivation; a small portion of it formed a kitchen garden, whilst the rest was sown with four kinds of grain, wheat, barley, peas, and beans. The air was full of ambrosial sweets, resembling those proceeding from an orange grove: a place which though I had never seen at that time, I since have. In the garden was the habitation of the bees, a long box, supported upon three oaken stumps. It was full of small round glass windows, and appeared to be divided into a great many compartments, much resembling drawers placed sideways. He told me that, as one compartment was filled, the bees left it for another; so that, whenever he wanted honey, he could procure some without injuring the insects. Through the little round windows I could see several of the bees at work; hundreds were going in and out of the doors; hundreds were buzzing about on the flowers, the woodbines, and beans. As I looked around on the well-cultivated field, the garden, and the bees, I thought I had never before seen so rural and peaceful a scene.

I have quoted this episode in full because there are so many interesting cottage details – the woodbine hedge, the old man's love of his bees, the abundance of honey, the plentiful grain.

The old countryman was prosperous because he had some land, was still strong and active and had no dependants. He grew nearly all his own food and the sale of his honey paid for all other needs. But a housewife of the same period with many mouths to feed would have had to practise all sorts of kitchen economies. She would know that treacle was cheaper than sugar and that salt, the cheapest of all seasonings, could be sprinkled instead of sugar on porridge and fruit. She might grow caraway (*Carum carvi*) as an alternative to bought spices, she might steep nasturtium seeds in vinegar as the cheapest possible pickle, and make apple-water as the cheapest refreshing summer drink. She and her children would collect wild vegetables and fruit for cooking – nettle-tops, hop-shoots, mushrooms, crab-apples, sloes, strawberries and blackberries.

Though there were certain universal elements in cottage cooking, there were also many regional dishes, and so staunch are regional traditions that some of the recipes given in the old cookery books are still local specialities today.

Cornwall always specialized in pasties and pies, sometimes made with meat, sometimes with pastry and vegetables only, perhaps leeks or cauliflower. Gooseberry sauce was traditional with mackerel. Cornish women also cooked wild vegetables not found in other counties, like sea-beet.

In Ireland peasant women made a dish of potatoes, cabbage and butter called colcannon, which we would call bubble-and-squeak. In the saffron-growing district of East Anglia there were saffron cakes, in Dorsetshire apple-dough cake, in Wiltshire lardy cake, in Yorkshire batter pudding, in Northumberland girdle cakes, and in Norfolk marsh samphire was picked on the salt marshes and cooked like asparagus. If one made a picture map of Britain to illustrate the local dishes no county would be left a blank.

Even the French have been known to admit that English country cookery can be delicious and I myself, who spent many childhood holidays in farms and cottages, remember that the food was excellent wherever there was a garden and enough money to pay for the extra ingredients. In the country, it is poverty which creates bad cooks; in the towns, it is more likely to be laziness. In my own country cottage today, I often feel inspired to make a jam, a cream cheese or a jar of chutney which I would never bother with in town.

6
Growing for Show

The cottage flower garden is by its nature a place for mixed planting. For centuries, many of the plants were collected wild, and were more useful than decorative, so that climbers, herbaceous plants and shrubby herbs were grouped in any way convenient to the housewife – probably honeysuckle over the door, a bed for physic herbs, and mint and thyme somewhere handy for cooking. Design was not considered.

But a totally different kind of gardening appealed to some cottagers from as early as the seventeenth century, the intensive cultivation of flowers to achieve perfection of bloom. These were called 'florists' flowers'. At first, the florists devoted themselves to a wide range of garden flowers, improving them by meticulous selection, but in the eighteenth century the number considered worthy of the florist's attention was drastically reduced.

As gardeners acquired skill in breeding stupendous flowers and marvellous new varieties, of course they wanted them to be seen, and florists' clubs were founded and flower shows held for the exhibition of choice plants and for the exchange of seeds and slips, knowledge and gardeners' gossip. The early florists' clubs, like modern horticultural societies, were authoritarian in their management – exhibition rules were strict and flowers had to meet exact and demanding specifications. For more than 200 years, through the seventeenth, eighteenth and nineteenth centuries, flowers were improved and re-improved, first by selection, later by hybridization as well, until the catalogue of varieties was enormous. Most of them are lost today. By 1770, there were over 1,000 named ranunculuses, and more than 500 double hyacinths.

From the beginning – probably because the florist's art was brought to Britain by artisan refugees, especially weavers, first from Flanders and later from France – this elaborate plant breeding was a speciality of the artisan. It was an ideal recreation for the cottage craftsman, whether in country or town. His garden was probably small, perhaps a mere backyard, and floristry requires time but not space. Unlike the agricultural labourer, whose work took him away into the fields, a weaver worked at home all day at his loom and he could give his treasures the intensive care they needed. Later, when the industrial revolution made the artisan's life increasingly grim and mechanical, floristry was more precious to him than ever, perhaps the only lifeline connecting him with the natural world. Certainly, there were some florists living deep in the country, and flower fanciers would tramp twenty miles each way to a show in the nearest town, carrying their blooms in pots fitted to a shoulder yoke, but the heart of the movement was in or near the towns, particularly in the north of Britain, in Lancashire, Yorkshire, Derbyshire, Staffordshire and Scotland, where the hills and dales held the homes of so many cottage craftsmen.

Florists' flowers, especially auriculas and tulips, were already popular in the seventeenth century, and a book on the subject, *The Florist's Vade Mecum*, by the Rev. Samuel Gilbert, son-in-law of the great gardener and gardening writer, John Rea, was published in 1683.

Protective equipment for florists' flowers, 1834.

Gilbert compiled a calendar of flowers which he considered garden-worthy, and his taste was reasonably catholic – the florist had not yet become a narrow specialist. He included violets, auriculas, crocuses, double and other curious primroses, hyacinths, narcissus, crown imperials, ornithogalum, tulips, fritillaries, wallflowers, anemones, ranunculus, columbines, irises, roses, lilies, sweet rocket, sweet williams, pinks, clematis, cyclamen, marigolds, and many more. But he was disdainful of many common country-garden plants which he regarded as rubbish, so that already a rift was beginning to show between the general gardener and the specialist. He wrote in cutting terms about the nice mixed garden of the country housewife:

> There is your garden mallows, double hollyhocks, snapdragons, toad-flax, foxgloves, thistles, scabious, mullen, fennel flower, bindweed, lark's heels, Canterbury bells, thorn apples, apples of love, garden lupins, scarlet bean, snails, caterpillars, oak of Jerusalem, and of Cappodocia, trifles adored by countrywomen in their gardens, but of no esteem to a florist, who is taken up with things of most value.

Gilbert's practical advice to his readers shows the high degree of skill which floristry required. He weighed the merits of one manure against another – there were different uses for horse dung, deer's dung, asses' dung, rotted sawdust and 'green slime of still water mixed with fresh earth', and he discussed protective coverings. All the early florists' flowers were hardy, but they required protection from rain. 'House them not' said Gilbert, but the florist was to cover and uncover them as needed, and give them plenty of air.

In the eighteenth century, the art of floristry boomed, and became a source of much social junketing. Clubs were founded in many parts of the country, and flower shows organized which became occasions for club dinners or feasts at the local inn. The earliest feasts of which we have dates were in the middle of the century, but I feel certain that some were held earlier, and that records will turn up one day. Members of a club paid a subscription to cover the costs of a show and the dinner which followed, and often a local gentleman would be patron and would provide prizes, usually silver cups, spoons or punch ladles, or copper kettles. Perhaps the gentleman's gardener would compete, but most of the competitors were artisans, and wherever there were weavers, or other home-based workers, they were likely to carry off the lion's share of the prizes.

William Hanbury, whose *A Complete Body of Planting and Gardening* was a major gardening book published in 1770, wrote:

> At these feasts let not the Gardener be dejected if a weaver runs away with the prize, as is often done; for the many articles he [the gardener] has to manage demand his attention in many places. A very small shower, which may come unexpectedly, when he is engaged in other necessary work at a distance, will take off the elegance of a prize auricula or carnation; whereas your tradesman, who makes pretensions to a show, will be ever at hand; can help his pots into the sun, and again into the shade; can refresh them with air, or cover them at the least appearance of a black cloud; and this will be an ease and a pleasure to him, and enable him to go to work with more alacrity.

Hanbury, who appreciated and was expert in every branch of gardening, was a strong supporter of the florists and their absorbing hobby.

I find the skill and care given by the artisans to their flowers very moving. The weaver at his loom watched his pots in the garden as a mother watches a baby in a pram through the kitchen window. If the day was hot, he hurried out to shade his plants; if a shower threatened, he went out to cover them; he saw that they had plenty of fresh air, he fed them expertly, mixing up all sorts of horrid feeds; he disbudded them at the crucial time. There were as yet no cool greenhouses, but the florist had a battery of contraptions to protect his plants: awnings,

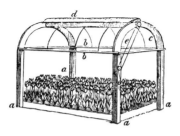

An awning for florists' bulbs, 1834.

umbrellas, oiled paper caps, glass frames and wooden canopies: the constructions were raised from the ground to keep out earwigs and worms and the pots were lifted on to tiers of staging when in bloom. Hence the alternative name of 'shed plants'.

While floristry became more socially popular, it became more horticulturally exclusive. By the end of the eighteenth century the number of flowers which the specialists accepted as worthy of inclusion in the canon was reduced to eight: anemone, auricula, carnation, hyacinth, pink, polyanthus, ranunculus and tulip. The auricula was the most difficult to grow, requiring rich and indeed obnoxious feeding. An auricula specialist called Isaac Emmerton, writing in 1815, recommended the following compost: two parts of goose dung steeped in bullock's blood, two parts of baker's sugar scum, two parts of night-soil, three parts of yellow loam, preferably the soil cast up by moles, plus two pecks of sand per barrow-load. Rival growers, perhaps nauseated by his recipe, claimed that Emmerton overfed his plants, which were short-lived.

The eight accepted florists' flowers were bred in such complexity that by 1798 there were 117 varieties of *purple* ranunculus alone, and one grower might have a thousand different polyanthus. The auricula had been bred to have a creamy 'paste' centre, the polyanthus had developed a gold edge to the petals and was called 'gold-laced'. The ideal flower had become something quite artificial, bearing little resemblance to the original type. For instance, every flower of top class had to consist of a smooth and perfect circle – the pink had lost its fringed edging and the tulip had lost its pointed petals and become a round cup. All petals, heights, markings, leaves and so on conformed to exact criteria. James Maddock, in *The Florists' Directory* of 1792, says of a fine hyacinth 'the stem should be strong, supporting numerous large bells, each suspended by a short and strong peduncle, or foot-stalk, in a horizontal position so that the whole may have a compact pyramidal form, with the crown, or uppermost petal, perfectly erect'. The other flowers were grown to equally strict criteria, making judging an exact performance. Judging today is rather more subjective, the judge's eye and taste playing a bigger part than angles, measurements and geometry.

By this date, the florist was not only following a tack quite different from that of the general gardener, but he was somewhat despised by the botanists, who, according to Hanbury in 1770, thought florists' work 'trifling, and beneath their notice'. This was unfair, because the florists were not attempting to be botanists, and some of the flowers they bred, especially the paste auricula and the gold-laced polyanthus, were wonderfully beautiful, and socially, the florists had created for themselves a competitive and exciting world.

That delightful person, the poet and parson George Crabbe, fully understood the florist's dedication, although he himself was a gardener of a totally opposite sort, a botanist and collector specializing, according to his son, in 'the rarer weeds of Britain'. Crabbe wrote of a weaver-florist who was also a student of insects:

> In vain a rival tried his utmost art,
> His was the prize, and joy o'er-flowed his heart.
> 'This, this is beauty! cast, I pray, your eyes
> On this my glory! see the grace – the size!
> Was ever stem so tall, so stout, so strong,
> Exact in breadth, in just proportion long;
> No kindred tint, no blending streaks between;
> This is no shaded, run-off, pin-eyed thing,
> A king of flowers, a flower for England's king!'

After 1800, the select list of eight accepted plants was expanded, and included tender flowers. The first important additions were the dahlia (the first non-hardy plant to be accepted) and the pansy, then came the chrysanthemum, the fuchsia, the sweet william, the iris, the cineraria, the phlox, the hollyhock, the verbena, the heath, the pelargonium (very important), and many more. For most plants, the circular flower was still the ideal, and a pansy, sprung from a heart's-ease with unequal petals, was bred to have five rounded petals forming a circle. The centre of pansy-growing was Derbyshire, where the cool climate suited its needs. Many districts had their own specialities – Paisley was celebrated for its laced pinks, Staffordshire for polyanthus, and the Lancashire weavers were, as they had always been, famous for their show auriculas.

From a wild pansy *(top)* florists developed circular flowers.

New florists' flowers meant new societies, and many were formed in the first half of the nineteenth century. Their shows were reported in the horticultural press, especially in Loudon's *Gardener's Magazine*, which noticed every kind of exhibition from the village show to the grand events in London; and then specialist journals were started, of which the most distinguished were *The Floricultural Cabinet*, which ran from 1833 to 1859, and *The Florist*, from 1848 to 1884. By this time, gentlemen, especially clergymen, and nurserymen had entered the florists' ranks and won many of the prizes, but the artisan had not lost his grip.

William Howitt* said that cottagers had a genius for certain pursuits

---

* It will be clear by now that I am a fervent admirer of this writer, who was much more balanced than Cobbett; he abhorred social injustice, but when he found happy corners of rural life, he appreciated them.

such as pigeon-fancying, bell-ringing, poaching, otter-hunting and angling, but that their three favourite hobbies were bee-keeping, floristry and natural history, especially the study of insects.

> This [floristry] is a taste full of beauty, and possessing a high charm, to select rich and suitable soils; to watch the growth and expansion of flowers of great promise; – it is sufficient for the enjoyment of one spirit.... Cottagers were among the first to raise fine flowers before floral societies and flower-shows were in existence; and the names of some of the village florists are attached to some of the finest specimens. Hifton, Barker and Redgate, appellations which some of our finest carnations, polyanthuses and ranunculuses bear, are those of old Derbyshire villagers well known to me, who scarcely were ever out of their own rustic districts, but whose names are thus made familiar all the country over.

I said in the last chapter that the peak of floristry was in the middle of the nineteenth century, and certainly it was hit hard by the grimmer aspects of the industrial revolution: air pollution, the advance of mass housing into the countryside, the transfer of the cottage artisan to the mills. But there was no abrupt collapse, and some of the societies continued to flourish until the end of the century, and new ones were formed and continue today. Roy Genders, in his book *Collecting Antique Plants*, puts the golden age of floristry as the century from 1802 to 1902. As late as 1879 an excellent book called *Hardy Florists' Flowers* was published, by James Douglas, but the eloquent introduction by a Yorkshire vicar, the Rev. Francis Horner, makes it clear that many florists' gardens were disappearing. 'Many of our busy towns, which, in the boyhood of men now middle-aged, had outskirt gardens, the familiar haunts of old florists, have spread their unlovely growths of bricks and mortar far beyond. It used to be a clear mile outside the town where in the earliest years of my florist life I grew auriculas and tulips; now, however, a raw and dreary street of monotonous tenements . . . overlies the old green spots.' And again this parson-florist looks backward to the time when the culture of florists' flowers was the delight 'of many a man in whom the love of nature was inborn and inextinguishable, but whose means were very spare, whose leisure was very scant, and whose advantages in pure air and light and garden space were poor and cramped'.

Flowers were not the only garden plants which roused the competitive spirit. Fruit and vegetables were cultivated for show throughout the nineteenth century, and the edible plant which roused the keenest rivalry was the gooseberry. Great was the gooseberry's girth and its weight was splendid. We are fortunate that records of the gooseberry shows in Lancashire, Staffordshire, Yorkshire, Derbyshire and Nottinghamshire from 1809 to 1895 have been preserved and have been edited in a delightful paper called *Gooseberry Shows of Old*, by R. A. Redfern (1944).

The shows were well organized, with presidents, stewards, secretaries and judges, and were accompanied by singing, solemn measuring and weighing, and, of course, refreshments and prizes; there were competitions between parishes as well as individuals, and prizes for maiden (first-time) growers, as well as veterans. There were usually three meetings a year, the first two on a Saturday in March and a Saturday in April, to choose the show date, make the arrangements and collect subscriptions, and the third was the big day, on a Saturday in early August. The show was held at a public house or inn, and the show of 1815 kicked off with the Gooseberry Growers' Anthem, to the tune

The gooseberry, favourite Victorian fruit.

of 'With Wellington, We'll Go, We'll Go'. Prizes were usually teapots or copper kettles, presented by the local gentry, and the experts collected them like golf cups.

The berries were of four colours, red, yellow, green and white, and of the winning varieties recorded throughout the nineteenth century, a few names occur again and again: Sportsman, Crown Bob, Huntsman, Yaxley Hero, Foxhunter, Wonderful, London, Ringer, Garibaldi, Leveller among others.

The heaviest berry ever recorded – the champion of champions – was in a match for ten shillings a side near Cheadle, Staffordshire, in 1852, and it weighed 37 dwt 7 gr., i.e. 37 pennyweight and 7 grains, which, mathematicians tell me, is just over 2 ounces, about the size of a small tomato. The variety was a famous gooseberry and frequent prize-winner called 'London'.

Though other fruits, and vegetables too, were, of course, regularly exhibited at flower and produce shows all over the country, the gooseberry, like the eight florists' flowers of the eighteenth century, was considered for a hundred years to be the worthiest fruit of all. This is confirmed by many references to it in Victorian literature in both history and fiction.

Today, gooseberry growing has declined considerably in the south of England, but not in the north, and one famous nurseryman in Yorkshire still lists more than fifty varieties of gooseberry in his catalogue. 'London' is among them, described as 'red, very large, round and smooth fruit. Delicious flavour when ripe.'

7

The Artist's Eye

As we saw with the Ladies of Llangollen, there were well-born romantics as early as the eighteenth century who were in love with the *idea* of cottage life rather than with the reality. The Ladies were to a certain extent playing a shepherdess charade.

A century later, in about the middle of Queen Victoria's reign, a number of artists – painters, writers, architects and gardeners – discovered a more genuine message in cottage life which has been important to us all. Most of them had no intention of living in small cottages themselves; but they discovered new values in country arts and crafts and in country serenity, and they cleared a path for the transition from centuries of property-worship and dreams of grandeur to the belief so strongly held today that small places can be beautiful. While the newly rich industrialist was making a stupendous mechanical garden in his country mansion or suburban villa, the artist reacted by turning to the old cottage garden as an ideal, and the cottage wreathed in honeysuckle, inhabited by a merry family contented with their peasant pleasures, became something of a cult.

The Painters

The cult of the cottage garden was initiated by Victorian painters perhaps a little before the writers arrived on the scene. Earlier landscape painters, like Constable, had seen cottages with the eyes of realism – dirty inhabitants,. ragged thatch, broken fences, tangling weeds – but from about the 1860s cottage painting took on a sunnier light. A school of water-colour painters of which Myles Birket Foster could be called the father, followed by Helen Allingham, William Stephen Coleman, Henry Sylvester Stannard, and many more, saw the cottage garden as a background to family happiness. In dappled sunshine, slender young mothers hang up their snow-white washing; pretty little girls in pinafores and sun-bonnets tend geese on the green; small boys go fishing with worms and a pin; there are halcyon hours of birds'-nesting and bluebell-picking; in the gardens, fruit-trees blossom and sunflowers peep over the hedge. Every picture tells a happy story, and the cottage garden has become an idyll.

Birket Foster was not, of course, primarily a cottage painter. Born in 1825, he started his career as a wood engraver and magazine illustrator, but in 1858 he turned almost exclusively to water-colours; his range of subjects over a long life was wide, including scenes of Venice and other cities on the Continent and of stately English country houses. But many of his pictures were tranquil rural scenes, with such titles as *Feeding Ducks*, *Children Going to School*, *The Little Nurse*, *Water-Lilies*, *Haycarts*, *The Shrimper*, *The Stepping-Stones*, *Hay Barges*, *Cowslip Gatherers*, *Rabbits*. His country people were all clean and neatly dressed, with contented, almost bovine, faces; the harvest was always good, the cattle healthy, the children helpful in their cottage tasks. The happy cottager of Victorian art had arrived.

Among his rural paintings, all beautifully composed and executed on a very small scale (many were 8 inches by 6 inches in size or less) were a number of cottages and cottage gardens. One of the most detailed is called *At Wheeler Street, Witley*, which was the Surrey village where Birket Foster lived, and shows a brick-and-timber cottage with diamond windows and a tiled roof and a rough garden inside a broken fence, with lilac, pansies, an Irish yew, a loosely clipped English yew, and a few clumps of flowers. The cottage is slightly tumble-down, though not dilapidated. When his friend and neighbour Lord Tennyson asked him 'Why do you painters always prefer a tumble-down cottage to others?' he answered, 'Because no one likes an unbroken line.' Birket Foster saw cottages as a painter, not as a social recorder.

His friend and successor, Helen Allingham, tells us much more,

because cottage pictures form the bulk of her work and, unlike Birket Foster, she was not a studio painter, but painted cottage gardens exactly as she saw them, finishing her pictures on the spot. The gardens and their flowers are recorded with rare fidelity.

Her first water-colours were painted in 1875 in London, where she moved in artistic and literary circles and knew Frederick Walker, A.R.A., whose work includes occasional cottage subjects, greatly admired by Ruskin, who wrote of a picture called *The Old Farm Garden*, 'it is worth all the Dutch flower pieces in the world'. She knew Ruskin himself, and Carlyle, Tennyson and Browning, and her husband, William Allingham, was the poet who perpetrated the immortal verse which begins, 'Up the airy mountain,/Down the rushy glen,/We daren't go a-hunting/For fear of little men.' In 1881 she and her husband and children moved to Surrey, and most of her cottage subjects are in Surrey or Sussex, though sometimes she moved farther afield. (Many of her paintings are reproduced in a biography of her by Marcus Huish called *Happy England*, published in 1903, and others in a later book by Stewart Dick called *The Cottage Homes of England*. Any cottage student will find both books well worth looking up in a library.)

Most of the cottages she painted are timber-framed with roofs of thatch, tiles or slate; they have broad, high chimneys and often diamond lattice windows, which were already becoming uncommon.

The gardens are usually in one or other of the two classic garden shapes. They either have tiny front gardens full of flowers and useful gardens at the side or back of the house; or they have a large front garden with a central path leading to the door, with flowers edging the path and vegetables and fruit behind the flowers. The garden is often surrounded by a picket fence, or by a hedge with a picket gate. One of the most charming features is the freedom with which the cottagers use the land outside the boundary. Sometimes geese and chickens stray on to the green, which is starred with wild flowers. Sometimes wild shrubs, like broom, growing on the bank outside, ramble into the garden hedge, while the garden lilac spills outwards. There is no tight

(Opposite) Through the eyes of artist Myles Birket Foster.

division between mine and thine. One feels that there is land for all.

Nearly all the cottages are covered with climbing plants. The commonest is ivy, which often covers the eaves and chimney, but there are also vines, Virginia creeper, roses and honeysuckle.

Fruit-trees are abundant, especially cherry- and apple-trees near the house, and one garden has a row of hop-poles. A large clipped holly bush is sometimes a feature, and there are often lilacs.

Of flowers, sunflowers and hollyhocks are the most conspicuous, either growing by the cottage windows or peering over the hedge. Tiger-lilies, madonna lilies, mignonette, lavender, sweet peas, sweet williams, peonies, wallflowers, snapdragons, all sorts of marguerites and daisies, shrub roses and dahlias are also identifiable. One large front garden with a central path edged with flowers is otherwise entirely filled with potatoes, which were by now the staple cottage vegetable. (Tess of the d'Urbervilles, returning from absence to her feckless father's home, found, to her dismay, that 'they had eaten all the seed potatoes – that last lapse of the improvident'.)

A faithful reporter, Mrs Allingham does not tidy up the gardens she paints. Some are well-kept, others are wild and weedy. The general picture of rustic happiness is not a fake, but the work of a painter who observed with tranquil eyes.

The Writers

While Mrs Allingham was painting her rustic scenes, some notable writers were praising the beauty of the cottage garden, and they admired it on two counts. Some saw it as a refuge for old-fashioned flowers, many of which had been driven out of garden after garden by the fashion for greenhouse-grown exotics and bedding-out. Others saw it as a model for garden design, with its simplicity of shape and reliance on hardy plants.

Mrs Ewing, author of *Mary's Meadow* (1883–4) and *Letters from a Little Garden* (1885) founded a Parkinson Society 'to search out and cultivate old flowers which have become scarce'. *Mary's Meadow* is a children's story revolving round the rescue from a cottage garden of an old hose-in-hose cowslip. In *Letters from a Little Garden* she tells us that

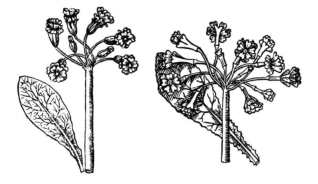

Hose-in-hose cowslip *(left)* and oxlip *(right)* were rescued from oblivion.

in the preceding decades gardeners at the big houses had flung herbaceous plants in dozens on to rubbish heaps to make way for bedding plants, and that the old flowers could be found in cottage gardens alone.

> It is such little gardens which have kept for us the Blue Primroses, the highly fragrant summer roses (including Rose de Meaux and the red and copper Brier), countless beautiful varieties of Daffy-down-dillies, and all the host of sweet, various and hardy flowers which are now returning . . . from the village to the hall.
>
> It is still in cottage gardens chiefly that the Crown Imperial hangs its royal head.

A few years later, Gertrude Jekyll, too, was to search cottage gardens for rare old roses and herbaceous plants.

In the same year that *Mary's Meadow* began to be published in instalments, 1883, William Robinson extolled the cottage garden for its natural planting and simplicity of style in *The English Flower Garden*, one of the most influential gardening books ever published. He had already written *The Wild Garden* in 1870, but I do not see much connection between wild gardening and cottage gardening except for the use of hardy plants. The later book was his first blast on this particular trumpet. Here, while attacking the rigidity and other shortcomings of the High Victorian garden, with its carpet bedding and clutter of statuary, he praised the cottage garden over and over again.

While the artist may be driven from the common bedding garden, he will perhaps go to rest his eyes on a cottage garden, and make a picture of it, as the cottage garden is itself often a picture. . . . Here is an engraving of a small cottage garden in Devonshire: an artistic garden in its simplest expression. There was very little in this beyond Roses and a few Pansies, and yet it was right and beautiful.

*   *   *

English cottage gardens are never bare and seldom ugly. Those who look at sea or sky or wood see beauty that no art can show; but among the things made by man nothing is prettier than an English cottage garden, and they often teach lessons that 'great' gardeners should learn, and are pretty from snowdrop time till the Fuchsia bushes bloom nearly into winter. We do not see the same thing in other lands. . . .

What is the secret of the cottage garden's charm? Cottage gardeners are good to their plots, and in the course of years they make them fertile, and the shelter of the little house and hedge favours the flowers. But there is something more and it is the absence of any pretentious 'plan', which lets the flowers tell their story to the heart.

*   *   *

Of the many things that should be thought of in the making of a garden to live in, this of fragrance is one of the first. . . . Apart from the groups of plants in which all, or nearly all, are fragrant, as in Roses, the annual and biennial flowers of our gardens are rich in fragrance – Stocks, Mignonette, Sweet Peas, Sweet Sultan, Wallflowers, double Rockets, Sweet Scabious, and many others. These, among the most easily raised of plants, may be enjoyed by the poorest cottage gardeners.

Many cottages are illustrated in this classic book, and it is noticeable that some of them are very large, more like manor houses treated in a cottage style. They are covered with creepers, have fruit-trees networked with roses, and are thickly planted with shrubs and flowers in a luxuriant mixture. By now the cottage garden has come a long way from the useful plot cultivated by the Elizabethan husbandman, or from the florist's meticulous little patch. Utility is being forgotten, luxuriance of planting is the ideal, with the garden a place of beauty not

(Opposite) William Robinson's ideal of a cottage.

only in spring and summer, but also in winter, when the garden relying on tender bedding plants would be quite bare.

Robinson's book, and also his articles in *The Garden*, moved innumerable well-heeled gardeners to replant their gardens in an informal style.

Another writer who loved cottage gardens and collected cottage plants was Mrs C. W. Earle, author of *Pot Pourri from a Surrey Garden*, published in 1897, when she was sixty-one. She has many memories of the cottage gardens of her youth and recalls conversations with old people whose memories went back to the beginning of the century. It is clear from her writing that the cottage garden was not highly thought of when she was a child, but soared much later in the esteem of connoisseurs. For instance crown imperials were fashionable, when *Pot Pourri* was published, for the first time since John Parkinson's day, for 'in my youth they were rather sniffed at and called a cottage plant'.

She is amusing on the subject of vegetables, saying how few were used by the average English cook, and that in London clubs, 'potatoes and Brussels sprouts represented in winter the whole vegetable kingdom'. In foreign hotels catering for English tourists only two or three vegetables were on the menu, to suit the English taste. (She also recollects that when she was young it was impossible to buy flowers in the streets or shops of the West End of London. This comes as a surprise to me, but I trust Mrs Earle's observation implicitly.)

Mrs Earle puts her finger unerringly on the best possible reason for taking up the cottage style even if you have the means for something grander:

> In gardening, as in many things in life, let your wits improve on what is rather below you; never look at the squire's garden in your neighbourhood, and then try and imitate it in small.

Though she was a connoisseur of cooking, flowers and hospitality, Mrs Earle's standards were always unpretentious.

The high priestess of the cottage cult was Miss Gertrude Jekyll, garden designer, writer, painter and photographer, collaborator in her early days with William Robinson and in her middle years with Edwin Lutyens, master of vernacular architecture. Country craftsmanship was in her bones, and the house which Lutyens built for her at Munstead Wood, Surrey, was of local stone and local oak, with gables and half-timbering, something of a cottage on a large scale. But the bulk of Miss Jekyll's garden designing was done in the twentieth century and was Edwardian rather than Victorian in feeling, so that her contribution to cottage-garden history belongs to a later chapter.

8
Working-Class Developments

Before looking at the large Edwardian gardens based on cottage ideals, one must turn aside for a last brief look at the cottager's garden at the end of the Victorian age, to see how it has changed since the days of John Claudius Loudon and William Howitt. Every county in England could now boast of picture-postcard villages with gardens with apple-trees, hollyhocks, sunflowers, mignonette and the other cottage favourites. They were cultivated by clergymen, doctors, minor civil servants, retired gentry, craftsmen, small farmers, labourers and independent gentlewomen, and all the other people who make up village society.

There was one important change in the style of gardening, and a number of developments. The major change occurred about the middle of the nineteenth century, when many cottage gardeners copied their richer neighbours and switched from mixed hardy planting to carpet bedding. This meant that they had to run up a small greenhouse, or at least a frame, to rear their tender plants, which would be planted out at the end of May or the beginning of June. The plants would die in the first frost, so the flowering season would be short, a drawback which the cottage shared with the manor house.

Such gardens were neat, brilliant in colour and eye-catching, and geometric beds and ribbon borders were planted with tropical or subtropical plants such as calceolarias, alternantheras, coleus, dahlias, echeveria, lobelias, verbena, begonias and ageratum. They were arranged in bedding schemes using the three standard components, carpet plants, edging plants and dot plants (these are taller plants, especially fuchsias, used as contrast to the small plants), and sometimes a pious motto, like GOD SAVE THE QUEEN, or the name of the cottage, was picked out in flowers. The meticulous cultivation of tender plants and their arrangements in intricate patterns gave many cottagers intense pleasure and pride, and the station-master and the lock-keeper, whose gardens were on show to the public, were often front runners and winners of local competitions. Towards the end of the century, the bedding fashion waned in large gardens, but it lingered on in many small gardens, especially in Scotland and the north of England, where they are still popular today.

The other changes in the garden scene evolved more naturally.

The Allotments

The official allotment system had got off to a slow start early in the nineteenth century. In spite of Acts of Parliament, many parish and even county officials remained indifferent to the cry for land and the number of acres given to allotments was pitifully small. But the private allotment system, with the labourer renting land from squire or farmer, gathered steam, the landlord often being stung into action by the exodus of labourers from the land. By the 1880s, many cottagers had allotments which stood between them and near-starvation. Some labourers reckoned that a quarter of an acre of land was worth two shillings a week on their wretched wages of ten or eleven shillings, which could drop even lower in bad weather. But others felt that

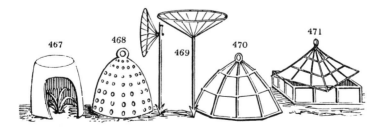

Protection for tender plants from frost and rain.

allotments were a sop to the labourers to prevent their demanding a living wage, and an allotment could be a burden to a man working on the land all day. Opinion was divided. The allotment, when provided and appreciated, was used for staple crops and the job of cultivating it fell to the man of the family.

The Victorian family, even in the working class, was founded on certain tribal conventions, and some tasks were 'manly' and others 'womanly' and other tasks again were restricted to the women and children. Though the cottage wives worked from dawn until dusk they did not work on the allotment, nor even cultivate the garden vegetables, but grew all the flowers and herbs. The children were not allowed to be idle; they gleaned corn for the fowls, collected snails and wild plants for the pig, scraped the roads regularly for dung, and sometimes picked up a few pence from the farmers by picking stones off the land or bird-scaring, but they had their garden compensations – they often had their own row of gooseberries or currants to gobble as they wished.

The staple allotment crop was the potato, and usually half the allotment was given to it; the other half might go to beans, carrots and parsnips, or to wheat for bread or barley for the pig, and in some districts potatoes, rhubarb and turnips were an accepted trio of crops. Fruit and choicer vegetables were grown in the garden, and all were grown to enormous size. Huge potatoes were aimed at and old-fashioned varieties grown – Ashleaf Kidney, Early Rose, American Rose, Magnum Bonum, known as 'magnum bonies', and the huge, misshapen White Elephant. Flora Thompson in *Lark Rise to Candleford*, her autobiographical novel of the 1880s, says

> Everyone knew the Elephant was an unsatisfactory potato, that it was awkward to handle when paring and that it boiled down to a white pulp in cooking; but it produced tubers of such astonishing size that none of the men could resist the temptation to plant it. Every year specimens were taken to the inn to be weighed on the only pair of scales in the hamlet, then handed round for guesses to be made of the weight. As the men said, when a patch of elephants was dug up and spread out, 'You'd got summat to put in your eye and look at.'

In Lark Rise, a fictitious name for the poor little hamlet on the borders of Oxfordshire and Northamptonshire where Flora Thompson was born, and where survival depended on hard work and thrift, 'every house had a good vegetable garden, and there were allotments for all'. But allotments still occurred only sporadically, even within a single county. In 1891, the *Daily News* published a first-rate series of eyewitness reports from a correspondent who was studying village life in the southern counties, and he found the standard of agriculture in Essex deplorably low. Then one day he came upon a village where the land teemed with produce. The allotments 'stood there like an oasis in a desert. The potatoes were certainly good, and every allotment was as full as it could hold of cabbages and beans, potatoes and carrots, onions and parsnips.' Probably there was a go-ahead squire or farmer who gave the men some leadership and perhaps started them off with seeds and plants, or perhaps there was a gardener of rare skill in the village who set the pace.

But in general there was justified discontent among the labouring cottagers, for wages were pitiful and many of the cottages which looked

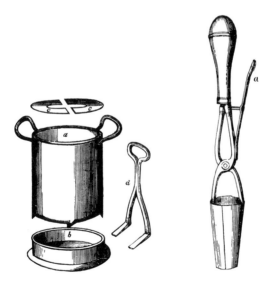

Tools for transplanting.

so picturesque to Helen Allingham were crumbling inside or dripped with damp or had a tainted water supply inviting cholera or typhoid. In quite a happy village, economy had to be so strict that a woman would make one Sunday bonnet last a lifetime and an engaged couple would walk to church in the morning to get married, walk home, eat a couple of chops as a wedding breakfast, change their clothes and go to work; and many villagers had never travelled more than a few miles from home.

Nor were the inhabitants of model villages invariably contented, for often comfort was bought at the intolerable price of loss of liberty. If the landlord was a stern paternalist the model village might be policed by bailiffs so strictly that the cottager 'could not sneeze without the bailiffs' permission'. They could make him tidy his garden, prevent his marrying, frown if his family were not regular in attendance at the church, or get him sacked for independent opinions. He could not even air his views freely in the village inn if the publican was the landlord's employee. At Lord Wantage's model estate in Berkshire, the villages were as exquisite as toy villages and the tenants had flower gardens and allotments. *But they were not allowed to keep a pig.* And though Lord Wantage, a staunch Tory, was not a man to exert improper influence on voters, it was remarkable that not a single Liberal voice was heard in his village. The *Daily News* correspondent remarked that the estate was 'a little political Dead Sea'.

The character of the landlord was still, as it had been for centuries, the overriding factor in village life.

Adventures with Plants: Vegetables and Fruit

The Victorian age saw an unprecedented explosion in plant material as explorers, nurserymen, seedsmen and private gardeners collected and bred new plants of every kind. Trees and shrubs, vegetables and flowers were grown in wondrous variety, and the cottage garden enjoyed some of the new wealth. I do not say that rare Japanese azaleas or the sensational new hybrid tea roses (the first was bred in 1868, a cross between a tea rose and a hybrid perpetual) became instant cottage plants; but cottage gentry were often among the keenest gardeners in

11 (opposite). The Victorian cottage cult attracted many painters and among the foremost was Helen Allingham. *At the Cottage Door* is typical of her tranquil approach, with a happy cottager in sun-bonnet and apron and a sprawl of beautifully painted cottage flowers.

12. One of the founding fathers of the cottage cult was Myles Birket Foster.
Usually his paintings showed the idyllic side of cottage life.

13. Sometimes Foster was more realistic. This tumbledown cottage has an untidy
garden with drooping cabbages; but there are roses and a vine on the walls.

14. William Stephen Coleman was another Victorian painter who idealized the simple life. Docile children, healthy vegetables and a burst of sunflowers suggest a prosperous world.

the country and would experiment with the new material, as it became more widely propagated and less expensive, and in a friendly village the small man would get presents of plants and could enlarge his range if he wished. Garden friends and rivals, seedsmen's lists and new books and pamphlets written *for* the cottage gardener and not *about* him also encouraged him to get out of the rut. The greenhouse gardener with his bedding schemes had already led the way, using introductions from tropical countries.

Taking food first, the cottage gardener had become less timid about vegetables. Celery, shallots, kohl-rabi, broccoli and, at long last, tomatoes became commonplace, and the gardener without a greenhouse or frame could buy cheap tomato plants and grow them on against a sunny wall. A few bold spirits tried Jerusalem artichokes, long resisted by the cottager, and endives. They also grew improved varieties of vegetables, even the humble parsley. 'Within the last score of years, this vegetable has been greatly improved in quality, chiefly through the efforts of competitors at horticultural exhibitions. In aiming to gain prizes for these plants, they have done their very best by selecting for seeding the very finest plants; so that now the parsley plants of the present day surpass, in the points of curl, crispness, and colour, to an immense degree the prize-plants of twenty years ago.' This was written in *Cottage Gardening* (1896), a splendid pamphlet by 'A Gentleman of Great Practical Experience'. He rates as the most important cottage vegetables potatoes, broad beans, runner beans, peas, onions, leeks and the usual brassicas, roots, salads and herbs. Beans ranked next to potatoes because 'every cottager has a pig' and beans and bacon had for centuries been linked together.

The Gentleman of Great Practical Experience was most anxious that the cottager should choose the right varieties of fruit, consulting his neighbours before buying fruit-trees to be sure the soil and climate were suitable. 'Pears of French or Belgian origin are in almost every case unfit for the cottage garden', but good new plums like Sultan or Czar should be tried, as well as the popular Victoria. Early plums were best for selling in the market, before prices dropped in the glut. Strawberries were the best small fruit provided the cottager had time to top-dress and water them and to cut off and replant the runners to increase

15 (opposite). The cottage gardens of the Edwardian gentry owed much to Miss Jekyll. Thomas Tyndale paints double herbaceous borders with flowering shrubs, roses and bright flowers offset by green and grey foliage plants.

The tomato came late to cottage kitchens.

his stock. He also favoured red currants, the best new variety being the American Fay's Prolific, white currants and raspberries for jam, especially the firm-fruited Fillbasket.

But gooseberries were his great enthusiasm. It seems impossible to overestimate the importance of gooseberries in Victorian cottage life.

> Gooseberries are good enough for a king ... two dozen bushes at least will not be too many for the average household. When green, they can be cooked; when ripe, what will more pleasantly refresh the palate in the hot days of summer, or what preserves can be expected to take the place of the jams prepared from the two sorts of gooseberries named Whinham's Industry or Red Warrington?

The author was clearly fond of children and thought that rows of small-fruited gooseberries, like Hedgehog, Green Walnut and Pale Amber, which fruited abundantly, should be grown specially for children.

In a well-run cottage garden the sale of produce was an important addition to income. Fruit, vegetables and honey were not the only saleable products. Some gardeners would grow a hazel hedge and coppice the bushes for pea-sticks and hurdles, and holly, nuts and flowers could be sold in the towns. One old man, whose family have owned their own cottage for several generations, told me, 'When we were children, we sold so many bunches of snowdrops in spring that they paid the rates.'

Adventures with Plants: The Flower Garden

Many new plants were finding their way into the cottage garden to join the old favourites. Old-fashioned roses, especially the very old *Rosa alba* Maiden's Blush, cabbage roses and moss roses were ubiquitous, as were sweet peas, lavender, hollyhocks, sunflowers, pinks, sweet williams, stocks, mignonette, honeysuckle, and all the rest. But new large-flowered delphiniums were finding a place, and dahlias in huge variety, and the poached-egg plant, *Limnanthes douglasii*, among the annuals, and *Clematis jackmanii* for the porch, and in the more ambitious gardens Japanese lilies, Japanese anemones, large hybridized irises, and the beautiful hybrid perpetual roses which dominated the Victorian rose garden from 1840 to 1890.

The hybrid perpetuals were bred from China roses, which have recurring blooms after the first flush, crossed with Portland, damask, bourbon or gallica roses. Most of them are very double, deliciously scented and come in rich reds from lilac to crimson and cottage gardeners grew them with enthusiasm and remained faithful to them when more fashionable rose growers had switched to hybrid teas. They can still be found in old cottage gardens today, and there are collectors who cherish them above all other roses.

Other new interests were plants with variegated leaves and rock plants. In the first case, carpet bedding, where foliage plants are essential, was perhaps the inspiration. In the second case, the big Victorian rockeries, often hideous to our eyes, prompted some cottagers to spare a sunny corner for a pile of rocks interplanted with small treasures. I myself know a cottage garden in Berkshire begun in the 1880s and passed down from father to son with very little alteration. There are four separate rocky places made of sarsen stones, three of them planted with rock plants and (curiously) pelargoniums; the fourth is a circle of stones enclosing a tiny pool, with goldfish and a water-lily. A small gnome keeps guard and looks perfectly appropriate.

Victorian window gardening, a rare art today.

Some of the new shrub introductions which were being collected and imported into Britain became cottage favourites, especially those which were not too large. The double *Kerria japonica* was a speciality, as was the flowering currant from North America, *Ribes sanguineum*, and other gardeners grew *Deutzia gracilis, Cotoneaster microphylla, Fatsia japonica*, skimmias, *Arbutus unedo* (the strawberry-tree), *Berberis darwinii*, and some of the conifers with which the Victorians were infatuated. The sizeable village where the squire and the parson lived was usually more go-ahead than the distant hamlet, as often cuttings of new plants could be obtained from the big house or the rectory.

The Window Garden

Window gardening is a cottage fashion which stretches back at least to Thomas Tusser who, in the sixteenth century, commended housewives to grow lilies, sweet williams, lavender, roses and double marigolds in windows and pots. Three hundred years later, this little branch of indoor gardening had grown prodigiously, and pot plants bloomed in the parlour window and porch of every cottage where flowers were loved.

Scarlet geraniums and the pink-and-purple fuchsia Rose of Castile were favourites, but there were often cactuses, an aspidistra, a hydrangea, a lily, or a pot of musk, 'either Harrison's mimulus flowering, or the old small-flowering, small-leaved sort with much better scent, or perhaps even the newer variegated sort'.* In front of the window, there might be a hanging pot or basket with the saxifrage *S. stolonifera*, known as Aaron's Beard. Most cottagers brought their plants outside in the summer to gain strength, and some displayed them on staging with a removable canvas cover, in the old tradition of the florists, to be admired by passers-by. Nearly all country writers of the period noted the flower-filled cottage windows with pleasure, often tended by very old ladies who were too rheumaticky, perhaps, to work out of doors.

The Eye of the Beholder

Social historians of cottage life towards the end of the nineteenth century tell us, rightly, a story of depression, poverty, bad housing, and an exodus from the farms. But a love of the country lies deep in the English character, and the many cottagers who survived the difficult conditions and patched their pretty homes and cultivated their small gardens contributed to making the English village of that time one of the loveliest places on earth. From the wealth of description by contemporary observers, none of them sentimental or dewy-eyed, I have chosen three quotations which bring the cottage garden into the mind's eye, and a final memory from Flora Thompson's *Lark Rise to Candleford*. This is not about the simple hamlet, Lark Rise, where she was born, but about the more sophisticated and prosperous village, Candleford Green, where she went in her teens to work as assistant to the Postmistress, Miss Lane, who was a family friend.

From a Correspondent of the *Daily News*, 1891:

> Here is a little place, just a few yards back from the highway, a semi-detached cottage. The windows full of flowers look out across the fields of

* *Cottage Gardening*, by A Gentleman of Great Practical Experience.

A cottage group in 1896.

waving corn, and pleasant meadows, and dark-green woods. Its doorway is sheltered by a porch that has been a mass of sweet-scented honeysuckle. Its forecourt garden is full of cloves and fuchsias, geraniums and sweet-peas, and under a canopy of old trees and shrubs is a rustic seat where, when the labourer's work is done, he may sit and smoke his pipe and watch the sunset, and see the evening primroses unfold. . . .

Here is another. A pebbled pathway edged by mossy stones leads up to it through beds of roses and petunias, nasturtiums and phloxes, interspersed with currant-bushes and raspberry canes. Its red-tiled roof and crumbling chimney stack stand picturesquely out against a background of plum and walnut, apple and pear trees, and its latticed windows peep cosily out of a cluster of vines.

From *Cottage Gardening*, by A Gentleman of Great Practical Experience, 1896:

It is now the month of June – leafy June as the poets call it – when the foliage forms so excellent a background for bright flowers. On the front of the cottage, which looks due south, is trained a healthy, free-growing climbing rose now in full bloom, the 'Yellow Glory', as cottagers call the famous Gloire de Dijon. . . . Below the high branches of 'Glory' on the east side and at the corner is a perennial pea already in bloom, and offering its pure white bunches as an effective counterfoil to the dimmed yellow hue of 'Glory' overhead.

Along the lines of the walk parallel to the cottage, as well as the centre walk leading from the highway to the cottage door, are numbers of sweet flowers standing alone, each a clump in itself, so well grown are they. Pyrethrum after pyrethrum stands erect beside its supporting stake, laden with scores of beautiful aster-like pure white blooms in one case, purple and rose in others; while the great peonies, the giants of the border, are one

110

mass of crimson or white. The double scarlet lychnis sends up a forest of spikes. The early summer roses usually found in cottage gardens are here in numbers ... the single yellow Persian rose, the double of the same variety, the Maiden's Blush, a most attractive flower; while a few hybrid perpetuals contribute their deep colours to the general effect.

Nestling on the ground are campanulas in blue and white ... sweet williams are opening their umbels of bloom to delight old-fashioned people who have admired sweet williams all their days ... pinks – white and pale pink – are one mass of bloom. When the harvest months are over, there is a display of dahlias and hollyhocks in every colour, and later on the Michaelmas daisies will have their turn in helping the show.

From *Old West Surrey*, by Gertrude Jekyll, 1904:

Cottage folk are great lovers of flowers, and their charming little gardens, in villages and by the roadside, are some of the most delightful incidents of road-travel in our southern counties.

The most usual form of the cottage flower-garden is a strip on each side of the path leading from the road to the cottage door. But if the space is a small one it is often all given to flowers. Sometimes, indeed, the smaller the space the more is crammed into it. One tiny garden, that I used to watch with much pleasure, had nearly the whole space between road and cottage filled with a rough staging. It was a good example of how much could be done with little means but much loving labour. There was a tiny greenhouse ... that housed the tender plants in winter. There were hydrangeas, fuchsias, show and zonal geraniums, lilies and begonias, for the main show; a pot or two of the graceful francoa, and half-hardy annuals cleverly grown in pots; a clematis smothered in bloom, over the door ... it must have given pleasure to thousands of passers-by.

From *Lark Rise to Candleford*, by Flora Thompson;

She had been in that garden before, but never in May, with the apple-blossom out and the wallflowers filling the air with their fragrance.

Narrow paths between high, built-up banks supporting flower borders, crowded with jonquils, auriculas, forget-me-nots and other spring flowers, led from one part of the garden to another. One winding path led to the earth closet in its bower of nut-trees halfway down the garden, another to the vegetable garden and on to the rough grass plot before the beehives. Between each section were thick groves of bushes with ferns and capers and

Solomon's seal, so closed in that the long, rough grass there was always damp. Wasted ground, a good gardener might have said, but delightful in its cool, green shadiness. . . .

Nearer the house was a portion given up entirely to flowers, not growing in beds, but crammed together in an irregular square, where they bloomed in half-wild profusion . . . the flowers grew just as they would in crowded masses, perfect in their imperfection.

9

Edwardian Afternoons

The click of croquet balls on the lawn. The murmur of flirtations by the lake. The rattle of epigrams and teacups round an elegant table laid under a spreading beech. And, ah yes, the swish of taffeta skirts on the path between the long herbaceous borders. The large Edwardian garden was a background for leisure, for the last of the idle days when a house-party might last for weeks and when even the young men-about-town fled to the country for August to pass the time indulging in lawn tennis or introspection. It was the dawdling world evoked by Henry James.

Herbaceous Borders

The Edwardian garden had its own characteristic features, of which the most celebrated was the herbaceous border. This was a speciality peculiar to Britain. Other Edwardian features – the pergola dripping with wisteria and rambler roses and the woodland garden with its rhododendrons and shrubs newly discovered in the East by E. H. Wilson and other great collectors – could be found in other parts of the world, but England alone has the perfect climate for herbaceous gardening. The John the Baptist of herbaceous planting, William Robinson, had preached his gospel well and gardeners all over England were turning his ideal into reality. Spires of delphiniums and verbascums rose through mists of lavender and santolina, clumps of tall daisies, lilies, achilleas, poppies, were thickly edged with leathery-

The doughty Miss Jekyll, aged nineteen.

leaved bergenias. Of all the herbaceous planters the most distinguished was Miss Gertrude Jekyll, who designed more than two hundred gardens in her long and successful life.

Her clients were people of substantial means. Herbaceous gardening makes high demands on labour, and the luxurious life of the English country house was underpinned by armies of servants, outside the house as well as in. A staff of thirty gardeners was not extraordinary (the great rosarian, Miss Ellen Wilmott, employed eighty-five at Warley Place), and quite a modest establishment with a garden of two or three acres would employ at least one gardener and a boy.

This may seem a far cry from the small cottage garden adjoining a farmhouse or on the village street, but there is a close connection. The cottage cult fostered by the Victorians was bearing fruit and for the first time in history the cottage garden with its mixture of hardy plants was exerting an influence on the gardens of the rich. The Edwardians did more than dally with picturesque cottage ideas, they seized and used them; cottage craftsmanship inspired many of Lutyens' houses and cottage planting was the foundation of the new flower gardens. Miss Jekyll herself wrote, 'I have learnt much from the little cottage gardens that help to make our English waysides the prettiest in the world. One can hardly go into the smallest cottage garden without learning or observing something new. It may be some two plants growing beautifully together by some happy chance, or a pretty tangle of mixed creepers, or something that one has always thought must have a south wall doing better on an east one.' Her herbaceous borders were the old mixed cottage borders writ large.

Of course, in upper-class circles, with all the resources of education and money, the border became highly sophisticated. Miss Jekyll's now legendary borders were planted with a painter's eye, so that every flower-bed made a picture.

In her own garden at Munstead Wood, the main border was two hundred feet long and fourteen feet wide, backed by an eleven-foot wall, with large drifts of flowers in harmonious colour schemes. At each end of the border the flowers were blue, white and yellow with grey foliage plants. These melted into groups of purple, white and pink flowers with more foliage plants, and the two met in the middle in a blaze of orange and red. Bold groups of yuccas marked the extremities and the herbaceous plants were mingled with shrubs, roses, bulbs, and tender plants like salpiglossis and tobacco plants. Her range of plant material was huge and she liked to mix homely lavender, catmint, pinks, grasses and wild soapwort with glorious lilies, tropical cannas, hybrid delphiniums and dwarf rhododendrons. The borders were meticulously staked and deadheaded and when gaps appeared in mid-season they were filled with greenhouse flowers planted in their pots. Some of her borders were in a single colour range, such as mauve and purple melting into white and grey.

The borders in smaller gardens were not usually as deliberate as Miss Jekyll's. Many were more genuinely cottagey with a tumble of old-fashioned flowers and fewer exotics. Sunflowers and hollyhocks, cottage lilies and pyrethrums, evening primroses and red-hot pokers, larkspurs and meadow-rue tossed about with a certain abandon, in a jumble of colour rather than a 'scheme'. Many such gardens were painted by contemporary artists like George S. Elgood and Beatrice Parsons, so that we know just what they looked like. One belonged to the Poet Laureate Alfred Austin who wrote a book about it called *The Garden That I Love* – a foolish, sentimental book, but with illustrations by Beatrice Parsons which show how delightfully cottage planting could suit a manor house.

Enjoying the Orchard

Another cottage feature which appealed to Miss Jekyll was the way in which fruit-trees, so pretty in blossom and in fruit, almost embraced the house, and she thought that the orchard of a large garden should be much more attractive and accessible than was the usual custom.

'Why', she wrote in *Wood and Garden*, 'is the orchard put out of the way, as it generally is, in some remote region beyond the kitchen garden and the stables? I should like the lawn, or the hardy flower garden, or both, to pass directly into it on one side.' She wanted the orchard, now in view from the pleasure garden, to be planted not necessarily in straight rows, but in groups or even groves, with medlars and quinces, Siberian and Chinese crabs, damsons, prunes, service trees and mountain ash, besides apples, pears and cherries, in both standard and bush forms. As the twentieth century advanced, many new orchards were sited and planted as she suggested, for instance at Sissinghurst.

A Return to Enclosures

The herbaceous border and the decorative orchard were not the only features of Edwardian gardens which drew inspiration from the cottage. Some important new gardens were made early in the twentieth century with a feeling of enclosure and intimacy which had not been seen in large gardens for hundreds of years. The garden of a manor house had usually been of partitioned design until the middle of the seventeenth century, but thereafter it expanded into straight vistas or sinuous landscape, then into the curved walks and shrubberies of the Regency, then into the open Italianate terraces and parterres of the Victorians. But the cottage garden (if it was cultivated at all) retained its hedges all the time, and can justifiably claim credit for the Edwardian revival of hedged and walled enclosures. The most glorious of the new intimate gardens was made by Lawrence Johnston at Hidcote Manor, in Gloucestershire, in 1905.

Hidcote is an amazingly versatile garden making the best of all possible worlds. There are vistas, borders, expanses of lawn, splendid trees, topiary, a stream, a woodland garden, fine steps and garden architecture, but the genius of the place is the series of small linked enclosures planted within the shelter of magnificent hedges. V. Sackville-West, who later made an equally great garden at Sissinghurst Castle in a similar style, was a friend of Major Johnston and knew Hidcote well. Nobody has ever described the garden with greater understanding.

> Would it be misleading to call Hidcote a cottage garden on the most glorified scale? (It covers ten acres, but acreage has nothing to do with it.) It resembles a cottage garden, or rather, a series of cottage gardens, in so far as the plants grow in a jumble, flowering shrubs mingle with roses, herbaceous plants with bulbous subjects, climbers scrambling over hedges, seedlings coming up wherever they have chosen to show themselves. Now in a real cottage garden, where limitations and very often the pattern – for example, the curve or the straightness of the path leading from the entrance gate to the front door – are automatically imposed upon the gardener, this charming effect is both restrained and inevitable ... it is very largely accidental. But in a big garden like Hidcote great skill is required to secure not only the success of the actual planting, but of the proportions which can best give the illusion of enclosure. . . . At Hidcote this has been achieved by the use of hedges. . . . In one such enclosure, I recollect, no larger than a fair-sized room, where moisture dripped and the paths were mossy and the walls were made of the darkest yew, scarlet robes of *Tropaeolum speciosum* trailed all over the hedges, more amazingly brilliant in that place full of shadows than ever it had appeared on the whitewashed cottage in Scotland.
>
> What I would like to impress upon the reader is the luxuriance everywhere; a kind of haphazard luxuriance, which of course comes neither by hap nor hazard at all.

Miss Sackville-West went on to explain that some of the plants, such as hydrangeas, peonies, primulas and fuchsias, were isolated in bold masses, but that far more were scattered and mixed.

> Generally speaking you are likely to find a patch of humble annuals nestling under one of the choicest shrubs, or a tall metallic *Onopordon acanthium* towering above a carpet of primroses, all enhancing the cottage-garden effect to which I have already referred. . . .
> There is just enough topiary to carry out the cottage-garden idea; just

117

enough, and not so much as to recall the elaborate chess-men at Hever Castle or tortured shapes at Levens Hall. The topiary at Hidcote is in the country tradition of smug broody hens, bumpy doves, and coy peacocks twisting a fat neck towards a fatter tail. It resembles all that our cottagers have done ever since the Romans first came to Britain and cut our native yew and box with their sharp shears.

Hidcote is a garden of surprise and variety, a garden of rare and magnificent plants, but it is the 'haphazard luxuriance' which sticks in the mind. There are flowers, and more flowers, and still more flowers, and if Miss Sackville-West saw it as a cottage garden, I think we can accept her view.

This seems the moment to discuss Sissinghurst itself. The garden at Sissinghurst Castle, in Kent, was not made until the 1930s, but it was almost the last of the great flower gardens of which Hidcote is a supreme example, for the luxuriant style waned with the First World War when the armies of gardeners melted away. Most large modern gardens are woodland or shrub gardens, and only the utter dedication of V. Sackville-West and her husband, Harold Nicolson, made Sissinghurst possible.

Sissinghurst, like Hidcote, is a garden of vistas with openings leading into romantically planted enclosures. These enclosures are called the forecourt, the tower lawn, the rose garden, the white garden, the cottage garden, the herb garden, and the orchard, and they are linked by a network of paths each ending in a statue, or a gate, or some other focal point of interest. There are also richly planted groves and banks, but the linked cottage-like enclosures are the heart of the garden. The orchard is the largest and is visible from the flower gardens as Miss Jekyll had suggested, and is planted with fruit-trees and groups of shrubs and roses, with many bulbs in spring and autumn.

Reading Miss Sackville-West's copious garden writing, three words occur over and over again, 'romantic', 'profusion', and 'cottagey'. The whole garden is lavishly planted, walls are latticed with climbers, rosebeds are underplanted with herbaceous things, shrubs have carpets of bulbs at their feet. Miss Sackville-West's taste in plants was catholic and it would be absurd to suggest that all her plant material was cottagey. She liked fine exotics from all over the world, especially those she brought from her travels abroad, and used many tender plants reared in the greenhouse. But she never lost her love of the simple flowers of the English countryside, and her garden was full of old-fashioned roses, scented flowers, herbs, cottage favourites like double primroses, violas, pansies and pinks, and herbaceous flowers from the Kentish woods. She loved self-sown seedlings, refused to have the hedges too tidily clipped, and allowed a mixture of climbing plants, like clematis with vine, to intertwine on the walls.

Her love of privacy, enclosure, and mixed planting in a simple layout was shared by Harold Nicolson, whose separate cottage at Sissinghurst looks on to the small formal enclosure called The Cottage Garden. Here small beds carved out of crazy paving are crammed with yellow, red and orange flowers, for Harold Nicolson liked what he called sunset colours.

Sissinghurst is the last cottage garden made on a grand scale, but fortunately it does not mark the end of cottage gardening. We are today in the middle of a great gardening revival involving every plant-lover from the botanist to the landscape designer, from the owner of a stately home to the commuter with a suburban patch. The cottage gardener is a natural leader of this grand movement, for the small garden is both numerically and artistically of the highest importance, and the cottage gardener has the advantage of combining practical knowledge with a sense of tradition.

10
The Cottage
Garden Today

The modern cottage garden does not slot easily into 'types'. There were no pressures on the old cottage gardeners to make sudden changes and many did no more than carry on their father's garden or copy their neighbours. A new plant might be introduced here, or a new technique adopted there, but in general gardens changed slowly and the motive behind them was constant – food production was the overriding necessity, and a few flowers were grown for pleasure.

Today, the pressures are different, and poverty is not dominant. Perhaps the strongest single force is the communications industry, which has produced a gamut of styles. The touring habit, the gardening press, television, flower shows, coloured catalogues and a stream of gardening books batter the mind with new images, and different gardeners will be receptive to different ideas. There may be a great mixture of styles within a single village or, in towns, on a single street. I know a terrace of Regency cottages in London's Chelsea with small front gardens each twelve feet by nine in size, all beautifully kept but all different. There are rose gardens, paved gardens, a dwarf conifer garden, a garden with a tiny lawn surrounded by bedding plants, and even a pot garden with spring bulbs, lilies, trailing pelargoniums and runner beans all grown in tubs and troughs. Every country village could show as much variety.

There are also new cottagers. Little old men with gnarled fingers scraping up 'taties' and apple-cheeked wives making corn-dollies and yarrow beer and walking ten miles to market are now quite hard to find. People of every class, income and profession have entered cottage life.

Townspeople, weary of the city grind, have moved into the country, travelling to town when they must, and as rarely as possible. Others are weekenders, and incur a little odium as such. Parents of young children buy a seaside cottage to solve the holiday problem. And country people of long standing do a general post; often the squire and his wife move from the manor-house into a cottage when their children are grown up and away and the big house has become too large. Of the original cottage population, the craftsmen have vanished; the agricultural workers remain, reduced in numbers, and are still the core of cottage society, though by no means the poorest part. So there is no such thing as a typical cottager or a typical cottage garden, with its topiary peacock and bower of honeysuckle and its teeming vegetable plot as a vital defence against hunger.

The only common factor is that people who like cottage life probably share a feeling for tradition. They may be alpine specialists, dendrologists, vegetable men, barbecue fanatics, pond gardeners, greenhouse experts, self-sufficiency freaks, collectors, botanists or plantsmen, but they probably feel that their garden must 'fit in' with the village scene. They are aware that certain flowers, colours and materials are appropriate to cottage gardens, while others jar. From the many latter-day cottage gardens I have seen I have chosen three for description as representative of today's mood. The first is a council-house garden very strong on vegetables, which are exhibited at shows and have won many prizes. The second is a plantsman's flower garden. The third is a weekender's garden. All three were made by the owners from scratch.

I must make a few general observations before describing these particular gardens. Taking the country as a whole, the design of an enormous number of cottage gardens has been altered to make room for a garage or open parking space inside the property. This usually means the loss of the traditional path to the front door. (This does not apply widely in town gardens, where cars are usually parked in the street.)

Secondly, the owners of productive gardens nearly always have a deep-freeze, and this is not confined to rich people. Thirdly, though vegetable growing is enjoying a boom in every locality and at every level, the keeping of livestock in a cottage garden is now uncommon. The backyard pig is too much trouble, and poultry are not a paying proposition unless the gardener can get free corn; if a cottager keeps a few hens or ducks, it is for fun. The fourth point is a continuation of a very old custom, the prevalence of barter. Many cottagers will give a local farmer a few hours help in rush seasons in exchange for all the potatoes they need or a load of manure, or a wife will make jam for two households in exchange for free fruit. So there is no need for one man (or woman) to grow everything. Finally, whatever Women's Lib may say, the old division of labour between the sexes still holds good; both men and women may be keen flower-gardeners, but where produce is grown for the kitchen, the men are growing the vegetables, the women tend the herbs.

These three gardens are real ones, accurately described, not idealizations.

A Council-House Garden

Mr Jim Webb lives in a semi-detached council house of solid, good-looking design built in 1921. The main door is at the side of the house and the garden of rather more than a quarter of an acre lies to the side and back. Originally a straight path with beds either side of it led to the door, but when Mr Webb moved in in 1936 he scrapped all this to make a driveway leading to a garage. There was still enough space for a good-sized flower-bed near the house, which is planted with roses, and the new footpath curls round this bed to the door.

Mr Webb is a magnificent gardener. His first job was as a gardener's boy and later he was sole gardener at a large house, but finding the pay too poor when he married and had a family, he took a job with the Wessex Electricity Board in 1936 and stayed until his retirement thirty-nine years later, in 1975. Gardening is a passion with him, and he works about six hours a day in his garden in the busy seasons, moving in winter to inside work in his three greenhouses. He inherited one old wooden dog-kennel house, bought a metal one several years later, 'and the third was a present to myself on my retirement'. This also is metal.

The garden soil is what he calls 'lacey', or patchy, part being loam, part light soil, all nearly neutral with a pH factor of about 7.0. The garden lies at the bottom of a hill, but is rather exposed and he says the soil is cold. The big vegetable garden behind the house is divided by a grass path; at the end is a flower-bed running across the garden; and there are several other flower-beds in strategic corners, surrounded by grass paths or lawn.

Mr Webb cultivates everything he grows to the highest possible standard, using the greenhouses to the full both for growing ornamental plants and as nurseries for starting the vegetables and bedding plants. All three houses are heated by electricity, two being kept frost-free at 45 degrees Fahrenheit, while the third is raised to 60 degrees for propagating in the early months of the year. Electricity at a cheap rate is a perk earned by retired electricity employees of long service, 'though, mind you, when they scrapped the old Wessex and made it part of the Southern Electricity Board, it was never the same. All the old personal touch was gone.' This garden is good all round, but its glory is the vegetables. These win so many prizes at local shows that they pay all the garden costs, Jim Webb's prize-money in an average season being about £14, or the same as his seed bill. His methods are as follows.

The Vegetables. 'One of the most important principles is the rotation of crops. I plan my garden in thirds and the crops are moved on in a three-year rotation. Green stuff usually follows potatoes, peas and beans follow the winter greens.

'I am a great believer in farm manure and I'm lucky, I can get it for nothing, and the whole garden is manured every year, except for the root crops – manure will cause carrots to fork. I might add a bit of Growmore to get things moving in the spring; the roses get some bonemeal or fertilizer in March; and of course the tomatoes get liquid feeds once a week in the growing season, but in general I don't buy bag manure. I make compost in two old oil drums, pushing the vegetable matter in at the top, activating it with Garotta, and taking it out when rotted at the bottom. I use it for the sweet peas and runner beans. I don't spray a lot and I do all the weeding by hand – the couch grass and bindweed are terrible here – though I use weedkiller on the lawns. Peat? No, there's no goodness in peat; I prefer to go out in the woods and collect some leaf mould for mulching.

'Another thing I don't hold with is a lot of watering. You have to flood the same ground over and over again to do any good; if you don't water all the time, the roots will come up to the surface looking for water. I prefer to keep hoeing.'

Mr Webb grows nearly every vegetable you can think of except globe artichokes and asparagus, which he doesn't care for, and celery, for which his ground is too cold; and he grows only a few rows of potatoes for exhibition because he can buy potatoes in bulk from a farm. But there are onions, shallots, peas, all sorts of beans, summer cabbage, winter cabbage, sprouts, leeks, purple-sprouting broccoli, sweet corn, beet, carrots, turnips, parsnips and a range of salads. One of his three greenhouses is devoted to tomatoes, of which he gives away at least 2 cwt every year. He starts picking fruit in early June and nearly every year can go on picking up to Christmas. He saves his own onion seed but prefers to post off a yearly order to a seedsman for the rest. Except for tomatoes ('one can't live on tomato purée'), all other surplus vegetables go into the freezer. 'We are completely self-supporting all the year round.'

Most of the vegetables are sown in the warmest greenhouse in January and February, starting with the onions, and are planted out in suitable weather in spring. The sweet peas are sown in January in the greenhouse, the bedding plants in March. Shallots, of course, go straight into the ground in February or March, as do the peas, in the third week in March if the weather is mild. 'And I never transplant lettuces. I sow two or three seeds together nine inches apart and thin the seedlings when they are big enough to eat. Transplanting lettuces checks their growth and makes them tough.' He was modest about his many prizes, which have made him a local celebrity, but, when pressed, explained how he wins them.

'I don't grow for show, I just pick out the best I have. Yes, it's true I have had up to fourteen prizes at one show and in my best year I won the President's Cup for the best exhibit and, I think it was, seven or eight other firsts as well. My speciality is the class for the best collection of five vegetables, four of each kind, for instance, four potatoes, runner beans, tomatoes, onions, carrots.

'It's not a question of size. Huge vegetables don't taste good and they don't win prizes. The vegetables must be perfect specimens, uniform in size and shape, and well presented.' Mr Webb does not use many tricks of the trade, though he puts a drainpipe over each leek to blanch it. I suggested to him that retired people, having time for gardening, perhaps carry off most of the prizes, but he says that the young people in his district are extremely keen. 'I can tell you, I have to keep my end up. The competition now is hotter than ever it was because there are more classes open to all comers, not just to members of the horticultural club, and exhibitors come from a long distance. Some of the younger men use rotavators, but I do all the work by hand.' He himself usually shows at four different local shows; his own village, combining with several other nearby villages, puts on a very fine show indeed.

The Fruit. Mr Webb has only three fruit-trees, all apples, two of them Cox's Orange Pippins and one a Bramley Seedling, but he grows a full range of soft fruit, including strawberries, currants, loganberries and raspberries; he does not go in for gooseberries, that speciality of the north. These are all in a fruit-cage made of posts covered with nylon netting which, although it is weather-proof, is removed in the winter. 'You must let the small birds into the cage in winter to pick up the grubs and beetles.' The surplus fruit is all deep-frozen.

Greenhouse Plants. Mr Webb is not a specialist and has never won more than a second prize. However, there are exquisitely neat rows of small pot plants in the cool house, such as cyclamen and *Lachenalia orchioides*, and some good pelargoniums and ferns.

Garden Flowers. He loves all flowers, especially scented ones and, apart from the rose-bed by the front door, there are several flower-beds in the garden with herbaceous plants and bedding plants mixed in a whirl of colour. Every year there is a fine row of cordon sweet peas sown in the greenhouse in January and planted out in spring. The roses are hybrid teas. A favourite herbaceous plant is an old-fashioned dark-red clove carnation, there are clumps of lavender, and bedding plants include *Salvia splendens*, lobelias, and all the old favourites mixed with perennial plants – there is no carpet bedding. There are bulbs in spring, with the scarlet tulip Apeldoorn in the main rose-bed, left in the ground, surprisingly, from year to year. There are only a few shrubs and the chosen ones all have scented flowers – a camellia, a *Daphne odora*, a ceanothus.

This cottage garden, so well cultivated, so productive, so pleasant to the eye and so sweet-smelling, brings modern advantages to the old tradition. Of the new aids used, electricity is the most important; but the owner still believes in hand labour in the open garden, and still enjoys that ancient stimulus to gardening, competition.

Another prize-winning gardener, this time in a Cotswold village with lime in the soil, confirmed most of Mr Webb's principles. Mr Freddie Jacques also dislikes rotavators, preferring to dig by hand, is insistent about rotation of crops, manures with farm manure and compost, and grows only a few potatoes because he can buy them from a farm. But he differs from Mr Webb in certain key respects. He saves a lot of his own garden seeds, especially sweet-pea seed. He leaves his nylon netting over the fruit-cage all the winter as a frost protection. And he is an enthusiast for seaweed manure, which he applies liberally as a pick-up feed every spring. As with Mr Webb, all surplus fruit and vegetables are frozen. His front garden has been cleared and gravelled for parking and turn-round space, though there are decorative features such as a background of shrubs, a small pool with goldfish, and a painted wheelbarrow planted with heathers.

Growing for Show Today

Mr Webb's success at horticultural shows leads us into the subject of competition gardening, which has never been more popular than it is today. There are more than 2,500 local horticultural societies affiliated to the Royal Horticultural Society, and many others which are independently organized. Some are new, but a few are as much as ninety or a hundred years old, founded when the old florists' clubs, centred on a public house, were dying out.

Today, interest is about equally divided between flowers and vegetables, but at most local shows there are many extra categories such as flower arrangement, homecraft, handicrafts, and even painting and photography. Men, women and large numbers of children are among the competitors, who are mostly amateurs – cottagers, allotment holders, retired people, weekenders and others – rather than professional gardeners. Interest is spread throughout Great Britain, though the north of England has obsessions of its own, such as gooseberries (coming up again strongly after a decline) and 'pot leeks', or leeks which are fat at the base instead of being straight.

Children's classes are a thriving section everywhere, and in the produce sections home-made wines are gaining ground, whether made from imported wine essences or from old-fashioned ingredients, like elderberries or parsnips. Most horticultural societies hold one show a year, probably in August, though there is a move towards a second, spring show. The big specialized societies, like the National Chrysanthemum Society, often hold two shows in their big season, in this case, the autumn.

The Royal Horticultural Society, to which so many societies are affiliated, publishes a guidebook for organizers, exhibitors and judges, and nobody who reads it can be in doubt as to what constitutes a good or a bad exhibit. For instance, onions should have thin necks and a parsnip should have good shoulders; carrots should be tender, of good shape and free from side-roots, the skins and colours clear and bright, size according to the cultivar. Size is not a merit in itself, and though it is possible to enlarge a vegetable to elephantine size, this would spoil the culinary value and would not take the grower nearer to a prize. It is possible to enlarge a marrow or pumpkin by making a small hole near the stalk and inserting a piece of string with the other end in a bowl of water – a sort of intravenous feeding – but the cooked marrow would make a mushy dish.

Like the doping of athletes or horses, certain practices are illegal. Produce should be carefully washed but not polished and all fruit, apples and pears as well as grapes and plums, should be shown with its natural bloom; bleaching potatoes to whiten them is *not* permitted, nor oiling a vegetable to make it shine. Flowers, of course, must also achieve perfection and uniformity, but many flowers, such as carnations, win points for fragrance, and arrangement is important.

The Horticultural Society to which Mr Webb belongs, the Burghfield and District in Berkshire, is characteristic of many prosperous and well-organized village societies elsewhere. The programme for its annual show in August, always a crowded event held in the village school, is proof of the great current interest in flower shows.

In a typical year, there are seventeen separate classes, some open, some for members only, some for novices, some for children. Entries are invited for such exhibits as: a collection of five vegetables; five pods of peas; ten runner beans; a pot of cactus or succulent; three different specimen roses; a vase of five pompon dahlias; a round flower arrangement for a dinner party; an article of crochet work; a 1lb jar of chutney; a bottle of home-made beer; six sausage rolls; a decorated hard-boiled egg (for children); a vase of hydrangeas, three stems. There are cash prizes in every class, usually £1 for a first prize, but more at a big show, and there are also coveted cups and bowls for top exhibits.

The judges at such events are highly skilled, some judges travelling from show to show to pronounce their verdicts. An average number of exhibits at a good show would be 400–500, entered by perhaps eighty to one hundred exhibitors.

There is another kind of competition open to cottage gardeners in certain districts, that is where the garden itself is on show and the judges go round from garden to garden or, it may be, from allotment to allotment. However, this is not so widely popular as the horticultural show, possibly because of the difficulties of judging gardens of diverse sizes and sites. This kind of competition is more easily organized in towns than in the country; civic authorities often give it their blessing, and there are prizes for different categories, such as front gardens, back gardens and window-boxes.

A Plantsman's Garden

One of the features of Colonel John Codrington's cottage garden in Leicestershire is a froth of cow parsley edging the shrubberies. The cow parsley is typical of the whole style of the garden, for it is a place where wild plants are treasured, and there are many native plants, both common and rare, naturalized in woodland or grass, and many plant species which John Codrington has collected in his travels all over the world.

I have said that there is no such thing as a typical modern cottage garden, for there are so many variants, but John Codrington does, I think, embody some important modern attitudes. His is a conservationist's garden, a collector's garden, and a sentimentalist's garden, as well as being delightful to the eye. It is also something of an eccentric's garden, for there are many plant oddities. It is not an exaggeration to suggest that John Codrington has the curiosity and the passion for variety which inspired the gardens of the Elizabethans. Hundreds of plants from native sorrel to rice (yes, rice) are grown within the space of one acre, and there are all sorts of garden conceits, from tubs of oranges and lemons under glass to an aviary.

Taking the conservationist aspect first, Colonel Codrington is anxious to grow, and to distribute among friends, some of our fast-disappearing English flora. Some years ago he collected, in an Essex hedgerow, seed of an umbelliferous plant widely thought to be extinct, *Bupleurum falcatum* (sickle hare's ear), and naturalized it. He grows the now rare oxlips, many wild geraniums including *G. phaeum* (dusky cranesbill), *Ranunculus lingua* (greater spearwort), *Anemone vulgaris* (pasque-flower), the rare hog's fennel, *Peucedanum palustre*, which is planted on the verges of his pond, and all three native mignonettes – *Reseda lutea*, *R. alba* and *R. luteola*. All gardening friends are encouraged to ask for seeds, roots or cuttings of his wild-flowers, to increase the chances of their survival. More common wild-flowers, like cow parsley, are naturalized in many parts of the garden, and buttercups, campion, columbines and many marguerites are encouraged in the orchard grass, while Solomon's seal, hellebores and *Smyrnium perfoliatum* make drifts in the woodland. However, John Codrington clamps down on coarse weeds like nettles, bindweed and ground elder.

The hundreds of foreign species in the garden of Stone Cottage bear witness to John Codrington's skill as a collector, and all are evocative of his world travels – he is one of those gardeners who find equal pleasure in growing plants and in the associations which the plants recall. As he walks round his garden he enjoys the *Smilacina* found in the woods of North America, the *Artemisia arborescens* from Agrigento in Sicily, the *Potentilla nepalensis* from Kashmir. Switzerland, Italy, India, Australia, Sri Lanka, Japan and South America have all produced treasures for him, and he hopes to continue travelling and collecting for the rest of his life.

The eccentric plants are the *jeux d'esprit* of a gardener whose interests are comprehensive. He has a tiny lean-to greenhouse, heated up to 70 degrees Fahrenheit, called his 'economic house', in which he grows commodities used in the household. His failures are tea and cloves, but sago, rice, coffee, cotton, cinnamon, nutmeg, vanilla, pepper and sugar are all to be found there. Nor is his herb garden conventional. Designed as a checkerboard, with squares of stone and earth, he grows a wide range of kitchen herbs, including liquorice, woad and alecost; but he also has a garden of poisonous herbs, with big red labels for safety, including monkshood and deadly nightshade.

I have stressed the wildness of John Codrington's garden because naturalization is the foundation of his philosophy and this appeals, I think, to the new generation of gardeners. But I must also give due credit to its excellent design. The garden of one acre is planned to seem much larger than it is, and the dull, flat garden he took over in 1952 has been broken up into a series of connecting features to create interest and mystery, joined by a maze of paths, and has been profusely planted. It is an inward-looking garden and until a few years ago was almost entirely enclosed by the garden vegetation, which grows fast in the rich soil of what used to be Rutlandshire. Then there came an extraordinary change in the surrounding country. A vast reservoir called Rutland Water was made a mile away, so of course John Codrington cut arches in the overhanging trees and shrubs to give views of the new man-made lake – an unexpected bonus in a garden already crammed with incident.

The small front garden of the cottage is traditional, with a central path to the door flanked by hedges of Hidcote lavender; there is lawn behind the lavender, and flower-beds under the front garden wall are planted with black and white tulips for spring and floribunda roses for summer – Queen Elizabeth and Copenhagen. The front of the cottage is covered with climbing roses, *Solanum crispum*, and a vine, and the beds under the windows, the only beds in the garden which face south, are planted with slightly tender bulbs like nerines and agapanthus.

Once you have turned through the iron gate at the side of the house, you are in the series of surprise gardens with their mixtures of simple and exotic plants. There is a stretch of orchard grass with old-fashioned roses and naturalized bulbs and summer flowers. There is a natural pond fringed with marsh plants like rodgersias, rheum, candelabra primulas and astilbes. Behind the pond a belt of trees and shrubs along the garden boundary is cleverly planted to seem like a whole woodland: it is laced with peat so that rhododendrons, camellias, *Rubus odoratus*, pernettyas and other calcifuges can revel in the woodland soil, and it is underplanted with wild-flowers and ferns. There is a white-and-grey garden; there is a gravel garden where self-seeded flowers inspired John Codrington to plant some of the scree plants he had collected abroad – asphodelus from Ephesus, *Bidens ferrulaefolia* (a composite plant) from Ecuador, and many more. There is the herb garden already described, and a vegetable garden, now neglected though John Codrington hopes to restore it.

One particularly successful piece of *tromp-l'œil*, increasing the apparent size of the garden, is the treatment of what was formerly a dull, rectangular lawn. Colonel Codrington divided it into two lawns by piercing it with a wedge-shaped shrubbery – at the point of the wedge stands a fine magnolia. All the shrub plantings include evergreens, especially behind roses which John Codrington feels need an opaque background all the year round. Honeysuckle and climbing roses twist their way through many of the shrubs.

Although the garden is cold and there is no natural windbreak, Colonel Codrington claims, between his cottage and the Urals, clever shelter planting enables him to grow many tender trees and climbers – *Fremontodendron californicum*, *Abutilon vitifolium*, myrtle, *Eucalyptus gunnii*, and an olive tree which is perhaps the most northerly olive in England.

He has a catholic taste in colours as well as in plants and thinks that one much-abused colour is orange. He broadcasts seeds of orange calendulas and coreopsis, likes orange and vermilion roses, orange daylilies and Siberian wallflowers. He is puzzled by the current anti-orange fashion and likes to recall the orange-and-black glories of the Russian ballet.

Not everybody's cottage garden, you may say. Indeed, John Codrington has heard so many visitors on open days complaining of the weeds that he now labels his cow parsley *Anthriscus sylvestris* to impress the ignorant. But his feeling for nature in his garden, his catholic taste in plants, embracing such diverse beauties as azaleas and buttercups, and his interest in culinary and useful plants, make him, in my view, a gardener in the mood of today.

Another of my favourite cottage gardens, in Beckley, Oxfordshire, is owned by a gardener with some of the same ideals, though the design of the garden is quite different. The cottage is built right on a village lane, and the whole garden of some half an acre lies behind the house – there is space in front only for climbing roses and honeysuckle. At the back, the ground drops down sharply below the cottage, and a winding gravel path with massed herbaceous borders on either side leads down into an orchard thick with bulbs and wild flowers.

The owner, Lady de Villiers, a graduate of Somerville College, Oxford, says:

> I was brought up on Helen Allingham's *Happy England*, and I always wanted a cottagey garden. I wanted roses and apple-trees, borders of mixed herbaceous flowers and narrow beds under the windows with clumps of polyanthus and pinks. I also wanted vegetables and fruit and, above all, flowers to pick all the year round for myself, for my friends and for the church.
>
> I also like to help to preserve the wild flowers which are disappearing so fast. The fields round here used to be full of green-winged orchids, cowslips and cuckoo-flowers and there were blackberries to pick in the autumn. Then the fields were ploughed and now the best wild flowers are in the cottage gardens. We have also planted primroses and periwinkles in the churchyard which have increased very well.

It is impossible to imagine a more romantic garden. Helen Allingham would have loved to set up her easel in the orchard and look up the garden path to the rose-smothered cottage at the top; but the view downhill from the cottage windows, looking over the tops of the flowers down to the apple-trees and quinces, with a view of the Oxfordshire landscape beyond is equally attractive. Tucked out of sight there is a good-sized patch of soft fruit and vegetables, so that the garden, contributing to the economy of the household, stands squarely in the cottage tradition.

One should not leave the subject of the garden of plantsmanship without paying tribute to the work of the late Mrs Margery Fish. Mrs Fish was not only a great plantswoman and plant collector but a woman who, through her marvellous books and lectures and her hospitality to other gardeners who made the pilgrimage to her home, revealed the world of cottage gardening to many who would never have heard of it without her.

Mrs Fish and her husband went to live in Somerset in 1938 and she died in 1969. In the years between she made, at East Lambrook Manor, a garden of cottage mixtures such as had rarely been seen before; exotic plants rubbed shoulders with simple double daisies, there were foliage plants in thousands, old-fashioned plants and even little weeds hallowed by their appearance centuries ago in Gerard's *Herbal* or John Parkinson's *Paradisi in Sole*. There were no vistas in her garden, nor landscaped features to be viewed from a distance. The design was a patchwork, perhaps on the 'bitty' side, but the harmonies of planting to be appreciated at close quarters were a joy. Now that labour is scarce and the grand manner must be left to the care of institutions, private gardeners turn increasingly from the big spectacle to the close-up beauty of plants. Mrs Fish's sort of gardening was exactly right for our time, which is why her influence has been deep and will be lasting.

A Weekend Garden

I have chosen my own garden to represent this very large category because I know it so well. I have owned the same cottage for more than forty years and I know every stick and stone in the garden; I sit under a mature walnut-tree which I planted as a nut, and I am on friendly terms with the woodlice which cluster under the aubrietas.

Weekenders, I know, are vulnerable to criticism, and I sometimes feel guilty at being only a part-time countrywoman; but as my husband is a Fleet Street cartoonist, four to five days a week in London are essential to us. I do not think that the village resents us, for we have lived there longer than most of the inhabitants and are part of the scenery, and we know everybody and join every possible event. I think it would be a sad day if town and country were to be split into two rival camps, with no mutual involvement, and if country people want to use goods produced in cities (and not many of them would care to reap corn by hand or dispense with television) it seems fair that city people should enjoy a share of the fields and trees. But I will stop protesting and return to the garden.

My garden, which I deeply love, is much too large for me, being more than one and a half acres; it is windy and cold, being 500 feet up on the Berkshire downs; it is very dry, sited on a chalk slope where the drainage is prodigiously fast. Assets are wonderful views in every direction; a good depth of topsoil in the old part of the garden round the cottage; and a number of mature chalk-loving trees – there were once many more, but we lost more than twenty elms to the dread disease. When I bought the cottage the garden was small, with a well, a tumbledown pigsty, a few old apple-trees and a jungle of weeds, for it had belonged to two old sisters in their nineties who died within a month of each other. But as the years went by I acquired extra bits and pieces of land when we needed a garage and the children wanted space to pitch a tent, play croquet, or let off air-guns to the terror of the village. I also tried keeping chickens, which laid remarkably few eggs. The final shape of the garden is wildly irregular, with irrational banks and ditches and some poor-quality, indeed useless, land on the perimeter. Today, the original small garden would suit me better.

The cottage itself is carved out of the slope so that there are steep banks at the back and sides. The front garden is small, with a path twenty feet long leading to the front door, flanked by box hedges. Behind the hedges are grass and shrub roses. The back door opens on to a flight of stone steps which lead first to the flower garden and then on to an orchard and island beds of shrubs, and beyond them, a croquet lawn. The flower garden is intended to be formal – a central grass path edged with flower borders has cross-paths leading to small separate gardens, four in all: a rose garden, a paved garden for outdoor meals, a

The author's weekend cottage.

vegetable garden and a shady garden with tall shrubs and lilies of the valley, campanulas and other woodland plants. But the formality of the design is something of a joke, because the slope is so steep and the site so irregular that no two things ever match. Even the hyacinths in pots on the steps can never be persuaded to flower simultaneously because one side gets more sun than the other. So the garden would be cottagey even if I wished it otherwise. In an average year, I am delighted with it in spring, pleased with it in early summer, and ashamed of it in late July and August, when it becomes a dustbowl. In autumn it picks up again and I love it in winter when it is weed-free and tidy and nestles under an eiderdown of compost and leaves. I have made quite a speciality of winter-flowering plants.

I am not putting forward my haphazard garden as any sort of model for others to copy, for it has glaring faults. I have chosen it only because it has taught me all the problems of a weekend garden and a good many of the answers, and when I fail it is largely because I have too much land. I consider the ideal size for a weekend garden to be anything from one-eighth to one-quarter of an acre, but even weekenders with such a manageable plot must bear in mind that their garden will be spending a lot of time on its own.

Extra help. The weekend garden must not become a tyranny, and if there is any chance of getting a few hours help in the course of the week, the weekender will seize it; I am lucky to have a pensioner one day a week. The priority jobs to be done in my absence are mowing and watering and my parting words are always 'whatever happens, Percy, mow the grass'. Nothing gives a better finish to a garden than mown grass, and nothing is more depressing than to leave a tidy garden on Sunday night and arrive the following weekend to find the lawn shaggy and spotted with dandelions. Selective watering is also essential, or one will lose plants in dry weather. Young plants, transplanted plants and plants in pots will need a drink between Sunday and Friday. If I had nobody to water, I would cut out pots altogether.

A Simple Structure. Here I speak from failure, not in the proud accents of success, for my garden is not labour-saving, and if I didn't have Percy I would simplify the design of the garden whatever the outlay. I would have brick paths instead of grass paths, would build a wall to enclose the front garden, replacing the old mixed country hedge which takes so much clipping, and lay paving instead of grass wherever possible; in short, I would replace the most labour-intensive plants (grass and hedges) with hardware. The cottage gardens of the Cotswolds and the Lake District always look beautifully neat inside their dry-stone walls, which can be embroidered with rock plants. If I ever make this change, I shall use the best possible materials – good bricks or cobbles and real stone, for texture is important to me. If I could find an old-fashioned craftsman, I would like my paths laid in a herring-bone or other traditional pattern, perhaps with sections of cobbles let into an attractive pattern of bricks. These changes would be extremely expensive, so I muddle on, but a simpler design would not

16 (opposite). Marigolds, poppies, hollyhocks and other traditional flowers in a Berkshire cottage garden.

17. A carpet of rock plants in a garden in Beckley, Oxfordshire, made by Lady de Villiers and described in Chapter 10.

18. An old man sits in a bower of honeysuckle outside his Cotswold cottage. In the foreground is a drift of sweet rocket.

19. Mr Jim Webb's superb vegetable garden, full of prize-winning produce, is described in Chapter 10.

0. Old apple-trees, a path of stepping-
tones, and clumps of pinks, lavender and
ther cottage flowers.

21. The most famous of all cottage gardens is
at Sissinghurst, created in the 1930s by Harold
Nicolson and V. Sackville-West.

22. Thomas Hardy was born in 1840 in this cottage in Dorset. The garden is planted
today with box, cotoneaster and other simple plants mentioned in his writings.

only save labour, it would be more attractive to the eye. Strong, simple outlines make the best background for mixed planting.

Good Weekend Plants. The planting of my garden is more successful than the design. I do not wish to bore the reader with long plant lists, but to suggest the *kind* of plants which suit a weekend garden. For five days a week the weekend gardener will be unable to water, hoe, spray or weed, so his plants must be good survivors. He will not want a punishing weekend, so his plants must be labour-saving. He will not want a garden which looks blowsy on arrival, so his plants must be neat and well-behaved. None of this implies a garden of coarse or boring plants. There are many beautiful and indeed rare plants which do not whine for constant attention.

The Born Survivors. Trees and shrubs are an obvious choice, and many weekend gardeners confine themselves to these alone. When our elms were felled I planted some hardwood trees as a matter of conscience, including a Turkey oak (*Quercus cerris*) and a weeping beech. I still water them in summer, but in a year or two they should be safely established. My other trees – a walnut, a chestnut, some field maples, an ash, a group of the lovely silvery-leaved *Sorbus aria lutescens*, a willow-leaved pear, and a few conifers – take care of themselves entirely.

Shrubs, of course, I have in multitudes and they give me no trouble at all. All they ask is an annual pruning after flowering, or a clipping-over in spring, and as pruning is the garden job I enjoy most I find my shrubs totally undemanding. I have a succession of flowering shrubs from the scented, pink-budded *Viburnum carlesii* of March to the winter mahonias, with *Spiraea arguta*, lilacs, deutzias, shrub roses, *Kolkwitzia amabilis*, various philadelphus, *Hypericum patulum* 'Hidcote' and many others in between.

But if most shrubs can fend for themselves, many smaller plants cannot long survive without human help except in heavy ground or a district with high rainfall. A weekend garden is likely to be a thirsty garden, with the hoe and the hose out of action for five days a week.

The best way of conserving moisture in the soil is certainly to mulch, and I try to blanket the sunnier beds in spring with compost and the

23 *(opposite).* Climbing Caroline Testout, an old-fashioned scented rose dating back to 1902, is underplanted with cottage pinks.

rosebeds with farm manure. But mulches have a way of disappearing, and in a dry summer shallow-rooted plants will suffer without water. I have regretfully given up such plants as phlox, bergamot and astilbes and concentrate on deep-rooting plants like achilleas, tansy, *Salvia superba*, Japanese anemones, acanthus, alchemillas, peonies and astrantias.

To mix with the deep-rooting herbaceous plants I use many rock plants and plants of the Mediterranean which will thrive in full sun: helianthemums, aubrietas, sedums, cottage pinks, cistuses, *Phlomis fruticosa*, and many euphorbias. My favourite cistus, *C. purpureus*, with crinkly pink flowers blotched with purple, has transformed a particularly dry bed in my garden, where a tall cypress robs the soil, into a well-filled corner.

Spring flowers, even water-loving flowers, do not present the weekend gardener with much of a problem, because both the soil and the atmosphere are cooler and damper than in summer. In shady places I grow many spring plants of the woods and streams: hellebores, lily of the valley, Solomon's seal, cuckoo-flowers, primroses, pulmonaria, oxlips.

Labour-saving Plants. This is a more controversial subject, because what is hard labour to one gardener may be pleasure to another. I love pruning and I like weeding, I loathe staking and I am terrified of ladders, so I am biased in favour of plants which do not need staking and climbing plants of moderate height. Since neither my husband nor Percy will go up one rung of a ladder, the sort of plant I do not want in my garden is *Rosa filipes* (of course, I have it), but younger, healthier gardeners may not mind spending Saturday mornings up a tree. However, most will agree with me that rampant climbers are not worth the trouble when so many equally fine plants can be grown which can be reached from a kitchen chair. I have learned over the years to think in terms of roses which grow to twelve or fifteen feet rather than thirty feet, and of clematis which I can tie and train in a matter of minutes on occasional Saturdays. I still have an 'Albertine' rose which I planted on the cottage front in my salad days, which is glorious for two weeks in the year, looks dreary after blooming, climbs to the chimneys and stops up the gutters. Today, I prefer shorter roses like 'Schoolgirl', 'Kathleen Harrop' or 'Golden Showers', or even the late-flowering Kordes roses like 'Elmshorn' and 'Dortmund'. I can just prune 'Étoile de Hollande' and 'Paul's Lemon Pillar' standing on a stool, but beautiful, strong-scented 'Madame Alfred Carrière' waves unpruned out of my reach. For the busy gardener the exuberant ramblers are just not practical.

I have been more sensible with my clematis. I uprooted my pink *Clematis montana* from the cottage wall years ago – it had become a tangle of dead leaves and old birds'-nests and flowered most freely on the roof. I planted in its place the lovely blue-flowered *Clematis macropetala* which grows to some ten or twelve feet. I have clematis in every part of the garden, especially the small-flowered species: yellow *C. orientalis* and *C. tangutica* and several varieties of *C. viticella*; my favourite is the green-and-white *C. viticella* 'Alba Luxurians', because I saw it in flower at East Lambrook Manor on my first meeting with that superlative plantswoman, Mrs Margery Fish.

I like all my climbers to be easy to control: self-clingers like *Hydrangea petiolaris*, or plants which mould themselves on to a wall, like *Cotoneaster horizontalis* and *Euonymus fortunei*. As a matter of sentiment I also grow the perennial pea, *Lathyrus latifolius*, because cottagers have grown it for hundreds of years.

Staking herbaceous border plants is a time-consuming job which can be reduced, if not eliminated; it is tedious with canes and string and pea-sticks are hard to come by. I grow a few favourite plants which need propping, like peonies and the orchid pink geranium with the dark eye, *G. psilostemon*, but more of the herbaceous plants which can stand without support. I am thinking of columbines, many campanulas, including the tall *Campanula lactiflora* 'Loddon Anna', *Aster frikartii*, nepeta, both the sturdy 'Six Hills Giant' and the more graceful *N. mussenii*, and decorative grasses like the striped *Phalaris arundinacea* var. *picta*, or Gardener's Garters. Very few of the hellebores need staking, though *H. corsicus* sprawls without a prop, but these are scarcely border plants – I prefer them among shrubs.

Plants of Neat Habit. A cottage garden is often sentimentally described as a natural paradise, but nature is in fact a messy gardener with a preference for rampant plants. In the garden I like nature well-tamed and look always for plants which grow in a tidy manner. This applies especially to hedging plants and ground-cover plants.

A good hedge pulls a garden together, and a slow-growing hedge always has more style than the tearaways. I have low box hedges in my front garden and taller yew hedges in the back garden, and I bless their stability. I also have, and love, a semi-circular hedge of hawthorn, one of the oldest of all cottage plants, with particularly fresh green leaves in spring.

On the other side of the coin I have old mixed hedges which are usually untidy, but as they were there when I bought the cottage I do not blame myself greatly for their presence. My great mistake was in planting a hedge of Leyland cypress when I wanted a boundary hedge in a hurry. This is a good plant when allowed to grow to its full height, but as a clipping plant it is a disaster, growing insanely fast and waving three-foot whiskers in the air a few weeks after cutting.

The weekend gardener should also be highly selective with his ground-cover plants. The rampant ones, like *Lamium galeobdolon* 'Variegatum' can smother a garden in a single year. I think ground-cover plants should either be neat and clumpy or, if one wants the creeping kind, should be easy to lift when they have outrun their allotted space. Clumpy plants which have served me magnificently are the epimediums, which have charming leaves as well as graceful little flowers, the sedums, most of them models of neatness, *Euphorbia polychroma* and *Alchemilla mollis*, though you must nick out the *Alchemilla* seedlings which will appear all over the garden. Many rock plants also make naturally tidy fillers, especially the helianthemums, *Iberis sempervirens* and *Saxifraga umbrosa*, or London Pride.

Of the creeping plants, I have several ajugas, or bugle, which can be forked out when they run too far, some manageable lamiums, and a carpet or two of *Anthemis cupaniana*, easily controlled with secateurs, but best of all are the hardy geraniums. *G. macrorrhizum* is an incomparable ground-cover plant – pretty little recurrent flowers, deeply lobed leaves which turn scarlet in autumn, and roots so shallow that you can pull out unwanted clumps with one hand. I like best the pink-flowered form called 'Walter Ingwersen'.

Other naturally tidy plants can be found among the herbs. Lavender, Jackman's rue, *Santolina incana,* and thyme (especially lemon thyme), chives and many varieties of sage are all beautifully well-behaved.

Bedding Plants and Annuals. My policy here is unconventional. It is usually said that annuals and biennials are too troublesome for the busy gardener, but I find them less time-consuming than the classic perennials like delphiniums and lupins.

True, there are several stages in the cultivation of biennials – sowing, lining out, and the final transplanting – but I am not too proud to let somebody else do the work for me. In short, I buy sweet williams, tobacco plants and Canterbury bells from a garden centre. Foxgloves sow themselves round the garden and it is remarkable how they always choose perfect places, perhaps at the foot of an apple-tree or in a gap between shrubs.

As for annuals, I find them no trouble at all. Some, like the poached-egg plant, *Limnanthes douglasii,* love-in-a-mist and annual borage, with pretty blue flowers for salads and drinks, sow themselves from year to year. I just push the seeds of other favourite annuals, especially clary, nasturtiums and lavatera, into the earth and forget about them until it is time to pick bunches for the house. None of my annuals need staking.

Vegetables. Fresh vegetables are a great treat and I have always fancied myself as a vegetable gardener; but they are hard work and the weekend gardener must all the time select and eliminate if his garden is not to become a burden. At the moment of writing I believe I have found the ideal solution to the vegetable problem. I have a friend in the village who lives in a converted schoolhouse with no garden and he is going to take over my vegetable patch. I am going to buy the seeds and manure and he is going to do the work. I will hoe and water in my spare time and we will share the produce. Whether this will work like a happy commune, or whether we will eventually hit each other on the head and dispute every runner bean, onion and cabbage, time alone will show.

I have written too much about my own garden. I hope I have suggested a few ways in which labour can be saved without loss of quality, but true gardeners will sometimes throw caution to the winds and grow difficult plants just because they love them. Nobody could call roses labour-saving plants, for they demand attention from pruning time to the end of the season, but I could not enjoy a garden without them. I will always grow sweet peas, even though I sometimes have to cut the pea-sticks myself in the hedges. I love the willow-leaved gentian, *Gentiana asclepiadea*, although it needs frequent watering in my dry garden. And I grow lots of irises, although they are magnets for weeds which pierce the very heart of the rhizomes; but most irises grow so magnificently in chalk that the reward is worth the labour. And for me the most treasured plants of all, whether easy or difficult, are those with happy associations – plants I have collected myself, plants I have propagated in my hit-or-miss way, and plants which have been given to me by my many gardening friends.

Epilogue

There have been attempts in the last few years to expose the tradition of the pretty cottage and its well-stocked garden as a myth, the argument being that cottagers have always been too wretchedly poor to cultivate a patch of land. It is suggested, in short, that the cottage garden is a sentimental fiction.

The motive behind this iconoclasm is laudable. Some social historians and, even more, architects who have studied village housing, feel that the sufferings of the rural poor throughout English history have been too little recorded, and that it is time to redress the balance. This attitude is high-minded, but in my view mistaken. If it is selfish to be complacent about the history of the peasantry, it is wilfully blind to see no charm or possibility of happiness in the old cottages and their gardens, for there is a great deal of evidence to the contrary. Taking the poems of John Clare alone, it is clear that many cottages and their gardens in the early nineteenth century were lovely and beloved. Clare, poor, lonely and melancholy, was not a man to see village life, or any other sort of life, in a rosy light.

I think the great flaw in English country life has always been the enormous power of the landlord; every rural community has been almost entirely dependent on one man's goodwill. But there have from the beginning been good landlords and bad landlords, and therefore rural prosperity has been patchy. There has been tragic degradation in cottage life and also, in some periods and in some places, decency and contentment. I hope I have produced enough evidence in this book to persuade doubters that the cottage garden, with its herbs and honeysuckle and its pig in the sty, is history, not legend.

Appendix:
Some Evidence on
Cottage Plants

The first serious reference to cottage plants is found in Chaucer, whose poor widow in the Nun's Priest's Tale grew, among other herbs, centaury, fumitory, caper-spurge, hellebore, spurge-laurel and ground-ivy.

Soon after Chaucer's death in 1400 a short treatise on gardening was written in English verse by Jon the Gardener, called *The Feate of Gardening*. A manuscript was discovered and transcribed in the 1890s by the great scholar of garden history, Alicia Amherst. Jon the Gardener lists nearly one hundred plants to be grown in gardens, most of them English native flowers, though there are a few foreigners and some common vegetables and trees. The poem is not specifically addressed to farm and cottage gardeners, but the list is unpretentious, and contains so many common wild-flowers that it gives a pointer to the contents of a modest garden. The list is:

Adderstongue (*Ophioglossum*), agrimony, alexanders (*Smyrnium olusatrum*), apple, artemisia, ash, avens, betony, borage, bugle, cabbage, calamint, wild celery, centaury, chamomile, clary, comfrey, coriander, cowslip, cress, daffodil, daisy, dittander, elecampane, fennel, field gentian, foxglove, garlic, goosefoot, gromwell, groundsel, hartstongue, hawthorn, hazel, henbane, herb Robert, herb Walter (Alicia Amherst could not identify this; it was a medieval name for woodruff, but this is placed elsewhere in the list), hollyhock (marsh mallow), honeysuckle, horehound, hyndeshall (unidentified), hyssop, iris, lavender, leek, lettuce, lily, liverwort, lychnis, mint, mouse-ear hawksweed, mugwort, mustard, nepeta, onion, orpine, parsley, pear, pellitory, periwinkle, polypody (a fern), primrose, radish, ratstail plantain, ribwort plantain, rose, rue, rye-grass, saffron crocus, sage, St John's wort, salad burnet, sanicle, savory, scabious, southernwood, spearwort, spinach, stitchwort, strawberries, tansy, teasel, thyme, tutsan, valerian, vervain, vine, violet, viper's bugloss, wall-pepper, water-lily, wood sorrel, sweet woodruff, yarrow.

With Thomas Tusser we are on our own ground. His *Hundred Good Points of Husbandry* of 1557, expanded into *Five Hundred Points of Good Husbandry* in 1573, was specifically written for small farmers and the book is highly practical. How the husbandmen, who were certainly illiterate, absorbed Tusser's worthy information, is beyond my power to guess – perhaps, as with ancient sagas, the words were learned by heart by travelling minstrels and chanted from farm to farm. Laying this problem aside, here are Tusser's extremely interesting lists of Elizabethan plants:

Seeds and Herbs for the Kitchen. Avens, beets, betony, bloodwort, borage, bugloss, burnet, cabbage, clary, colewort, cress, dock, endive, fennel, french mallow, goosefoot, leeks, lettuce, liverwort, long beak (?), lungwort, marigold, mercury, mint, nepeta, onions, parsley, pennyroyal, primrose, rosemary, saffron, sage, sorrel, spinach, succory, summer savory, tansy, thyme, violets, winter savory.

Herbs and Roots for Salads and Sauce. Alexanders, artichoke, asparagus, cress, cucumbers, endive, mint, musk, mustard seed, purslane, radish, rampion, rocket, sage, sea holly, skirret, sorrel, spinach, succory, tarragon, violets. To buy: capers, lemons, olives, oranges, rice, samphire.

Herbs and Roots to Boil or to Butter. Beans, cabbages, carrots, gourds, parsnips, pumpkins, rape, rouncival peas, turnips.

Strewing Herbs of All Sorts. Balm, basil, camomile, costmary, cowslips and paigles, daffodils, sweet fennel, germander speedwell, hop, lavender, marjoram, maudlin, pennyroyal, red mint, roses, sage, santolina, tansy, violets, winter savory.

Herbs, Branches and Flowers for Windows and Pots. Amaranthus, *Asphodelus albus*, bachelor's buttons, bay, campion, clove pinks, columbines, cornflowers, cowslips, daffodils, dianthus (wine-red spotted white), eglantine or sweet brier, feverfew, flag iris, french marigolds, hollyhocks, larkspur, lavender, lilies, lily of the valley, marigold, nigella, pansies or heartsease, pinks, rosemary, roses, snapdragons, star of Bethlehem (*Ornithogalum umbellatum*), stocks, sweet rocket, sweet williams, violets, wallflowers.

Appendix: Some Evidence on Cottage Plants

Herbs to Still in Summer. Betony, dill, endive, eyebright, fennel, fumitory, hop, mints, plantain, raspberry, roses, saxifrage, sorrel, strawberries, succory, woodruff.

Necessary Herbs to Grow in the Garden for Physic. Archangel, betony, chervil, cinquefoil, cumin, dittander, gromwell, hartstongue, horehound, liquorice, lovage, mandrake, mugwort, plantain, poppy, rhubarb, rue, saxifrage, stitchwort, sweet cicely, valerian, woodbine.

John Parkinson's *Paradisi in Sole, Paradisus Terrestris* (1629) is the first great book about pleasure gardening, and Parkinson wrote for well-to-do people. However, in his section on the kitchen garden, the following vegetables are mentioned as food for the poor: beans, globe artichokes, marrows, mint, onions, parsley, peas, radishes, savory, thyme, turnips.

John Worlidge, in his *Systema Horticulturae* (1677) has an interesting chapter on 'vulgar flowers' grown by farmers' wives. I have not seen this quoted before. He lists:

Aconites, apple of love, bachelor's buttons (a double-flowered buttercup), balsam apple, bellflowers, blew-bottles (cornflowers), candytufts, champions, cranesbill, crowfoot, dame's violet or queen's gilliflowers (sweet rocket), double chamomile, double daisies, double featherfew, double lady-smocks (cuckoo-flower), double pellitory, flower of the sun, foxgloves, grove-thistles, hollow-root (corydalis), marsh marigold, monkshood, moth-mulleins, nigella or fennel-flower, nonsuch or flower of Bristol (*Lychnis chalcedonica*), pilewort (lesser celandine), princes'-feather or common amaranthus, satten-flower (honesty), scabious, thorny-apple, toadflax.

In 1683 the Rev. Samuel Gilbert, son-in-law of the fine gardener and gardening writer, John Rea, published *The Florist's Vade Mecum*, giving lucid instructions for growing a wide range of garden plants. They were taken month by month, as a garden calendar. However, Gilbert was not writing for the cottager, so I shall not use his plant lists here, not did he mean by the word 'florist' a flower breeder, of whom there were so many in the artisan class. He meant simply an expert flower gardener.

There is a considerable gap in our knowledge of new cottage garden plants in the eighteenth century. Many excellent gardening books were written, but there is not much specifically about the humbler garden until the end of the century. (I exclude the garden of the Ladies of Llangollen as being much too grand.)

In 1792, we get a list of florist's flowers. James Maddock in *The Florists' Directory*, which the author claims to be the first serious book on the subject, states that there are only eight accepted florists' flowers: anemone, auricula, carnation, hyacinth, pink, polyanthus, ranunculus and tulip. In 1794, Sir Uvedale Price in *An Essay on the Picturesque* gives honeysuckle, vines and jasmine as cottage climbing plants, and recommends fruit-trees trained on cottage walls; and Britton Abbot of Tadcaster (1797) recommends, in fruits, apple, greengage, plum, apricot, gooseberry, currant, and adds potatoes to the usual vegetable list.

From 1800 to 1860 evidence on cottage plants is abundant. From the essayists and poets of the early part of this period I have chosen John Clare (1793–1864) as the best representative. He was himself a peasant and had a wide knowledge of flowers, birds, insects and all natural things. I have listed only the garden plants mentioned in his poems (or as many as I could find), not the wild-flowers. His plants of the cottage garden are:

Flowers. Aconite, columbine, cowslip, crocus, crowflower, daisies, everlasting pea, geranium, gilliflowers (clove pinks), golden rod, heart's-ease, hollyhocks, iris, larkspur, love-lies-bleeding, marigold, monkshood, pansies, red and yellow primroses, ragged robin, ribbon grass, roses (especially cabbage roses and sweet brier), snapdragon, sunflowers, sweet peas, woodbine.

Vegetables and Fruit. Broad beans, runner beans, pumpkin, black currant.

Herbs. Agrimony, balm, lad's love (artemisia), lavender, lavender cotton (santolina), marjoram, mint, parsley, rue, sage, self-heal, tansy, thyme.

Trees and Shrubs. Box, elder, hawthorn, holly, laurel, lilac, poplar, willow, yew. yew.

At the same period we get cottage plants recommended in an authoritative source. John Claudius Loudon in *The Manual of Cottage Gardening and Husbandry* (1830) and, with his contributors, in *The Gardener's Magazine* (1826 to 1843) lists:

Vegetables. Cabbage, carrots, cauliflower, cos lettuce, cucumber, Indian corn, leeks, onions, parsnips, peas, potatoes, radishes, runner beans, spinach, Windsor beans. Loudon also suggests home-grown tobacco.

Fruit. Apples, cherries, currants, gooseberries, peaches, pears, rhubarb, strawberries, (grape) vines. Rhubarb, recommended for tarts, is something of an innovation in cooking; its use for many centuries had been medicinal.

Flowers. Brompton and ten-week stocks, carnations, picotees and other pinks

pinks are mentioned, but it is assumed that cottagers will grow other flowers of their choice.

In 1840 a book called *The Amateur Florist's Guide*, by John Slater, was published, and by now the florist's flowers had increased from eight in number to twenty-one. They are: anemone, auricula, calceolaria, carnation, chellaston tulips, chrysanthemum, cineraria, dahlia, fuchsia, German China asters, gladiolus, hollyhock, hyacinth, pansy, pelargonium, pink, polyanthus, ranunculus, rose, tulip, verbena. The author also has a chapter on spring bulbs, giving a large variety, all species, including ten scillas and four fritillaries, including the crown imperial, which we know was at this time a cottage speciality. The author says in his bulb chapter, 'all in the above list are easily obtained and cheap, mostly from 2d. to 6d. a dozen'. John Slater does not mention heaths, but by 1850 they had become a florist's flower, as had irises.

In 1849, the first number of a magazine specially for the cottager, *The Cottage Gardener*, edited by George W. Johnson, was published. Many cottage plants are discussed in a practical way, and we get a substantial list of hardy perennials 'well suited for the amateur or cottager's mixed flower border', which I will give in full.

Vegetables are much the same as in earlier sources, except that there is more interest in celery and broccoli. Fruits and herbs are as before. There are some new annuals, *Eschscholzia californica, Clarkia pulchella, Nemophila insignis*, and increased emphasis on bedding plants and edgings for formal beds. Edgings include box, daisy, dwarf gentians, heath, thrift, and the following China roses are listed for bedding in groups: Adam, Baronne Delaage, Camellia Blanc, Cramoisie Supérieure, Duchess of Kent, Eliza Sauvage, Fabvier, Fulgens, Mme Goubalt, Mme Plantier, Mrs Bosanquet, William Jesse.

The nomenclature and spelling of the following hardy perennials are as given in the magazine:

For Spring: Adonis vernalis, Alyssum saxatile, Anemone appenina, Arabis saxatile, Aubrietia deltoides, Cardamine pratensis pleno, Gentiana acaulis, Hepatica triloba, Iberis sempervirens, Orobus vernum, Phlox divaricata and *P. verna, Phyteuma orbicularis, Primula vulgaris alba pleno, Pulmonaria virginica, Pulsatella vernalis, Tussilago alpina.*

For Summer: Achillea ptarmica flore pleno, Anthericum lilastrum, Antirrhinum majus, Aquilegia vulgaris, Bellis perennis pleno, Betonica grandiflora, Caltha palustris pleno, Campanula carpatica, C. glomerata, C. grandis, C. persicifolia, C. trachelium, Chelone obliqua, Convallaria majalis, Coreopsis lanceolata, Delphinium barlowii, Dianthus aggregatus, double sweet william, *Gentiana septemfida, Hesperis matronalis, Iris germanica, Lupinus polyphyllus,* various white peonies, *Paeonia officinalis, Penstemon gentianoides, P. coccinea, Phlox brightoniana, P. candidissima alba, P. omniflora, P. elegans, Potentilla macnabbiana, Spirea trifoliata, Trollius europaeus.*

For Autumn: Anemone vitaefolia, A. japonica, Aster amellus, A. elegans, A. novae angliae, A. pulchellus, A. pulcherrimus, A. spectabilis, Chrysanthemum arcticum, Liatris squarrosa, Matricaris grandiflora, Oenothera serotina, Phlox tardiflora, P. wheeleriana, Pyrethrum uliginosum, various rudbeckias, *Solidago lanceolata, S. altissimum.*

Finally, a list of window plants from an article in *The Cotage Gardener* of 1857 (the range is enormous and some contemporary authorities questioned the viability of some of the plants for house culture, e.g. erica, but the author states confidently that all can be raised in the house with the protection while germinating of panes of glass or even thin calico, and we know that the Victorians were very skilled with house plants):

1. Plants of a shrubby nature: Acacia armata, A. grandis and *A. drummondii, Cassia corymbosa, Coronilla glauca, Cytissus proliferus* and *Attleana, Dolichos lignosus,* ericas of sorts, fuchsias of all sorts, *Jasminum odoratum, Kennedya rubicunda, Passiflora coerulea, Sollya heterophylla.*

2. Plants of herbaceous character: Alonsoa incisifolia, Anomatheca cruenta, calceolaria, cineraria, *Chrysanthemum indicum, Campanula pyramidalis* and *C. nobilis, Cobaea scandens, Commelina coelestis, Cuphea platycentra* and *C. miniata, Gazania rigens,* Gladiolus, Liliums, Maurandyas of all sorts and colours, Mimulus, *Nierembergia gracilis* and *N. filicaulis, Oxalis rosea,* Pelargoniums, *Salvia coccinea, S. patens,* etc., *Schizanthus* Graham, *Sparaxis tricolor, Tigridia pavonia.*

3. Small annuals suitable for window decoration in summer and autumn: Anagallis phillipsii and *A. monelli,* Balsams, *Calandrinia grandiflora, Clintonia elegans* and *C. pulchella, Didiscus coerulea, Isotoma axillaris, Linum grandiflorum, Lobelia speciosa, Mesembryanthemum glabrum* and *M. tricolor,* Portulucca of sorts, *Rhodanthe manglesii, Acroclinium roseum, Primula sinensis fimbriata.*

4. Annuals for planting out in May for balconies and small flower gardens: Abronia umbellata, Amobium alatum, Antirrhinum, *Argemone grandiflora,* Aster (Chinese, French and German), *Bartonia aurea, Brachycome iberidifolia,*

Calliopsis drummondii, Datura ceratocaula, Dianthus Indian pink, Picotees and carnations, *Eschscholzia tenuifolia,* Helichrysum, Ipomaeas, *Lupinus mutabilis,* Lobelia, *Myosotis azoricus, Nolana atriplicifolia,* Penstemons, Petunias, *Phlox drummondii,* Salpiglossis, *Saponaria calabrica, Sanvitalia procumbens,* sedums, stocks, *Tagetes lucida, T. patula* and *T. erecta,* Tropaeolum, Verbenas, Zinnias of the *elegans* group.

List of
Illustrations and
Acknowledgements

9. Fritillaria, from Jane Loudon, *The Ladies' Flower Garden of Ornamental Bulbous Plants*, 1841, plate 52. (Photo: Tony Othen)
10. Tulips, from Jane Loudon, *The Ladies' Flower Garden of Ornamental Bulbous Plants*, 1841, plate 50. (Photo: Tony Othen)

Section III (between pages 104 and 105)

11. Helen Allingham (1848–1926). *At the Cottage Door*. Private collection.
12. Myles Birket Foster (1825–99). *Cottage at Amersham*. Courtesy M. Newman Ltd. (Photo: Medici Society Ltd)
13. Myles Birket Foster (1825–99). *A Cottage Garden*. British Museum.
14. William Stephen Coleman (1829–1904). *A Cottage Garden in Summer*. Christopher Wood Gallery. (Photo: Cooper-Bridgeman Library)
15. Thomas Tyndale (1855–1943) *Cottage Garden in Astley Down, Worcestershire*. Water-colour. $14 \times 10\frac{1}{4}$ in. Christopher Wood Gallery. (Photo: A. C. Cooper Ltd)

Section IV (between pages 136 and 137)

16. Cottage garden, Aldworth, Berkshire. (Edwin Smith Archive)
17. Cottage garden. (Valerie Finnis)
18. Old man's cottage. (Valerie Finnis)
19. Mr Webb's garden. (Eric de Maré)
20. Small garden. (Valerie Finnis)
21. Cottage garden, Sissinghurst, Kent. (Harry Smith)
22. Thomas Hardy's cottage, Higher Brockhampton, Dorset. (C. M. Dixon)
23. Climbing roses. (Valerie Finnis)

BLACK-AND-WHITE

Endpapers: Blaize Hamlet cottages. City of Bristol Museum and Art Gallery.

Frontispiece: Garden scene, from T. Price, *Modern Gardener*, 1826. (Photo: BBC Hutton Picture Library).

Page 11: Cottage with animal pen. Museum of English Rural Life, University of Reading.

Page 15: Pompions, from Gerard, *The Herball or General Historie of Plantes*, 1579. British Museum (Natural History).

Page 16: Snapdragons, from Gerard, *The Herball or General Historie of Plantes*, 1579. British Museum (Natural History).

Page 19: Potato, from Gerard, *The Herball or General Historie of Plantes*, 1579. British Museum (Natural History).

Page 103: Tulip and flower transplanters, from J. C. Loudon, *An Encyclopaedia of Gardening*, 1834 ed.

Page 106: Tomato, from Vilmorin-Andrieux, *The Vegetable Garden*, 1885 ed.

Page 108: Window garden, from *The Cottage Gardener*, 1849. Royal Horticultural Society Lindley Library. (Tony Othen)

Page 110: Engraving from *Cottage Gardening*, 1896. Royal Horticultural Society Lindley Library. (Tony Othen)

Page 114: Miss Gertrude Jekyll. Drawing by Mary Newton published in Francis Jekyll, *Gertrude Jekyll*, 1934.

Page 135: The author's weekend cottage, sketch by Osbert Lancaster. (Author's collection)

Page 144: Rustic chair for the sedentary man, from *The Florist*, 1849. Royal Horticultural Society Lindley Library. (Tony Othen)

Index

Figures in *italics* refer to the illustrations

Index